lib·er·tar·i·an *n* (1789) **1** : an advocate of the doctrine of free will **2** : a person who upholds the principles of absolute and unrestricted liberty of thought and action

"This book by Rev. Opitz will go a long way to help those in mainline churches appreciate the critical importance of liberty in the construction of a just society. It will disabuse all readers of the notion that to be a libertarian, one must be a libertine."
— FR. ROBERT A. SIRICO
    ACTON INSTITUTE FOR THE STUDY OF RELIGION AND LIBERTY

"The Reverend Opitz has long been, and remains, one of the most articulate and deeply thoughtful defenders of a free society. All that he says and writes, including the wisdom that infuses this book, is worth careful reflection."
— DONALD J. BOUDREAUX
    THE FOUNDATION FOR ECONOMIC EDUCATION

"The breadth of Edmund Opitz' knowledge and clarity of his thought make The Libertarian Theology of Freedom *a valuable handbook for those who prize God's own freedom, granted by Him for our use."*
— THE RT. REV. ROBERT C. HARVEY, BISHOP
    ANGLICAN CHURCH OF NORTH AMERICA

THE
LIBERTARIAN
THEOLOGY
OF
FREEDOM

by

The Reverend
Edmund A. Opitz

HALLBERG PUBLISHING CORPORATION
Nonfiction Book Publishers – ISBN 0-87319
Tampa, Florida 33623

ISBN Number 0-87319-046-7

Library of Congress Catalog Card Number 99-072105

Copyright © 1999 by Hallberg Publishing Corporation

Cover design and typography by Michael X Marecek.

Printed in the USA. First printing September 1999.

For information concerning Rights & Permissions or other
questions contact:

HALLBERG PUBLISHING CORPORATION
P.O. Box 23985 • Tampa, Florida 33623
Phone 1-800-633-7627 • Fax 1-800-253-7323

*Dedicated to the Remnant and the furtherance of
"the bond of joy" through which "the called and
chosen spirits are kept together in this world."*
— QUOTED BY ALBERT J. NOCK
AUTHOR UNKNOWN

Acknowledgements

The writings of Edmund A. Opitz
selected for this book stating
THE LIBERTARIAN THEOLOGY OF FREEDOM
were chosen from three books by
Reverend Opitz. These are:

THE POWERS THAT BE

THE KINGDOM WITHOUT GOD

RELIGION: FOUNDATION OF A FREE SOCIETY

We thank the respective publishers of
these books for their cooperation.

Contents

FOREWORD

In today's world, the term "libertarian Christian" seems to many people to be an oxymoron. It is not. It exemplifies nothing less than the true meaning of the teachings of Jesus.

Can we learn from the past? If so, this book containing writings of Reverend Opitz, some written over 40 years ago during the "Social Gospel" debate, should help "libertarian" Christians state their beliefs and reclaim their heritage.

Collectivism, under all its names – socialism, fascism, nazism, communism and increasingly under the name of Democracy – derives its support from what Albert Jay Nock termed "Epstean's Law." That is:

> "Man tends always to satisfy his needs and desires with the least possible exertion."*

And, what could be easier than using government to have someone else pay your bills? Or, for business to use government to limit competition and liability? Or, banking to gain a monopoly?

It is very tempting to use the power of the State to gain privileges. The one and only thing that held this temptation in check

---

*This is why well-intentioned government programs are abused and fail. It is why democratic governments become dictatorships as mass-man votes against private property rights and for "free services and benefits."

On the other hand, it is the driving force behind the invention of every labor saving device or machine since the invention of the wheel and, therefore, highly beneficial when directed by a competitive free-market economy based on the right of private property and equality before the law.

during the early years of our nation was the religious convictions of the majority of the people, as reflected in the Constitution.

Theirs was a highly individualist, "libertarian" religious concept that looked upon collectivist dogma with disdain.

In the mid-1800's a tidal wave of European collectivist philosophy and theology swept across the Atlantic which, by the late 1800's, became known as the "Social Gospel" under whose spell our individualist theology became branded as "selfish," "greedy" and surely, un-Christian.

Thus it was that the avariciousness of man, his desire to gain much and do little, delegated power to the State under the guise of "doing our Christian duty" to help our fellow man.

When the essays in this book were written, libertarians had no voice in mainline Christian publications, there were few libertarian book sellers, no libertarian political movement and few Evangelical Christian television and radio programs.

It is our hope that today the marketplace has changed to the degree that libertarian Christians will learn of this book. And that the information contained herein will prove both meaningful in their lives and help them explain their libertarian Christian beliefs to others.

CHARLES HALLBERG
PUBLISHER

PREFACE

The seeds of the Social Gospel took root in the optimistic atmosphere of the nineteenth century conquest of the vast American continent and its abundant natural resources. Man was rapidly becoming the master of nature, aided by the new mechanical inventions which were creating both an industrial and an intellectual revolution. Men everywhere were embracing two new congenial dogmas, that progress was inevitable and that man was essentially good.

These two doctrines became the fundamentals of the Social Gospel and the impetus to a shift in faith from God to man, from eternity to time, from the individual to the group, individual conversion to social coercion, and from the church to the state. The main inspiration of the new movement was non-Christian, and from the beginning it drifted readily into doctrines increasingly removed from biblical faith.

THE NEW GOD AND THE NEW JERUSALEM

The pagan origin of the Social Gospel was from the beginning apparent in its readiness to sacrifice Christian faith to the new order. As early as 1873, for example, the Unitarian, Octavius Brooks Frothingham, published *The Religion of Humanity*, dismissing altogether any faith in God in favor of the new god, man. His challenge, although premature, revealed clearly that the drift was from God to man, and that the new dogma would be preserved through sacrifices in theological faith. Collective man and his society were the new god and the new Jerusalem.

A bewildering array of reform movements and experiments in communal living were the order of the day. Believing in the perfectibility of man and human society, men were certain that heaven on earth was in their grasp if only certain social changes were made. An important contribution was made to this new thought by Jacksonian Democracy, and the utilitarian dogma of the "greatest good for the greatest number." Every reformer was confident that he knew what was the "greatest good" for everyone else.

THE GOSPEL'S MAINSPRING

In its motivating conviction this early nineteenth century mania for reform differed from the Social Gospel of a later date. It believed firmly in the dignity of the individual in a moral universe. However, a reaction against this individualism was already in the making.

In 1847, Horace Bushnell, Congregational clergyman of Hartford, Connecticut, neither an evangelist nor a reformer, published *Christian Nurture* in which he applied the environmentalism stemming from John Locke to religious experience. Instead of converting the individual by evangelism, Bushnell argued, children should be molded by a religious environment. Apart from the obvious fact that children should be taught religion, this was the beginning of an idea that formed the core of the Social Gospel. Instead of the converted individual changing his environment, a changed environment was supposed to convert the individual. It is not difficult to conclude from this, the Social Gospel viewpoint, that the environment, not the individual, is responsible for human behavior.

Twelve years after *Christian Nurture*, Charles Darwin's *Origin of Species* put a substantial foundation stone in the coming edifice of the Social Gospel. The Puritan tradition leaned toward science, and by the 1880's the majority of the clergy in this tradition had adjusted their thinking to Darwinism. They drew from the Darwinian theory the optimistic conclusion that an immanent God was at work in history evolving by slow process the Kingdom of God on earth. This furnished the Social Gospel with its philosophy of history.

AWAY FROM INDIVIDUALISM

The individualism that had tempered the strong sense of community imbedded in the Puritan tradition did not down easily. In spite of Horace Bushnell's *Christian Nurture*, the rank and file of the clergy of the 1880's still expected to affect society through the regeneration of individuals. They were suspicious of centralization of power, and of control by the state. However, individualism was showing signs of erosion, and the suspicions of the state were to be modified.

The rising materialistic spirit following the Civil War worried sensitive church leaders, and one of the most distressed was Washington Gladden, champion of Horace Bushnell's environmentalism. In 1885, Gladden attended a conference at Saratoga, New York, that introduced him to the idea of using the force of the state to achieve the social righteousness for which his heart yearned. This was not new. The Puritans had had their theocracy, but this conference placed the idea in a new context, and made the possibilities of the "Positive State" very alluring.

The conference included such notables as Simon Patten, Edwin F. A. Seligman, Edmund J. James, John Bates Clark, Richard T. Ely, Andrew D. White and Woodrow Wilson.[1] Some of these conferees were fresh from graduate studies in Germany where they had become enamored with Bismarck's use of the state in the area of human welfare. None was more influential in Ameri-

---

[1]During President Wilson's term the Constitution was radically amended. Popular election of Senators replaced appointment by their State. Direct Federal taxation of citizens, the "Income Tax Amendment" was declared in-effect even though not radified by a majority of States (*The Law That Never Was*, 2 vol. Benson & Beckman). And, The Federal Reserve System was established confiring a monopoly on US banking and credit to its 12 privately owned, member banks. (*Secrets of the Federal Reserve*, Eustace Mullins). Ed.

can Protestantism than Professor Richard T. Ely who directed much of his writing toward the church. A leader in the criticism of laissez-faire economics, he sought to persuade liberal Protestants to support him in his demand for more state intervention in economic and social life.

A ready pupil of Ely, Washington Gladden spoke on "Christian Socialism" at the 1889 council of Congregational churches. "It begins to be clear that Christianity is not individualism. The Christian has encountered no deadlier foe during the last century than that individualistic philosophy which underlies the competitive system."

Yet, Gladden was not a Socialist, nor were many of his colleagues at this time. He was trying to teeter in a position between individualism and non-individualism. Josiah Strong, another exponent of this nameless drift away from individualism, expressed his fear and disapproval of socialism in *Our Country*, published in 1885. The clergyman said: "Socialism attempts to solve the problem of suffering without eliminating the factor of sin."

THE MOVEMENT IS NAMED

As early as 1889, the Society of Christian Socialists was formed in Boston to "show that the aim of socialism is embraced in the aim of Christianity." William Dwight Porter Bliss, Episcopal clergyman influenced by Henry George's *Progress and Poverty* and Edward Bellamy's *Looking Backward*, organized this society including about twenty clergymen representing the Baptist, Methodist, Congregational, Unitarian, Universalist, Episcopalian and other denominations.

Reverend Bliss published *The Dawn*, a monthly journal which in its first issue stated: "Business itself today is wrong . . . it is based on competitive strife for profits. But this is the exact opposite of Christianity. We must change the system . . ."

Populism was the political fad of the West in the 1890's, and Iowan George D. Herron, Congregational clergyman, seized the opportunity to advocate Christian Socialism in the name of re-demptive love. So dynamic and persuasive was he that he won the support of a wealthy widow who used some of her capitalistic "plunder" to endow a chair for him in "Applied Christianity" in what later became Grinnell College.

Another Congregationalist, Reverend Ralph Albertson, put Herron's theory into practice by founding the Christian Com-monwealth Colony at Columbus, Georgia, in 1896. It attracted the sympathetic interest of Tolstoy, but went the way of all such experiments in communal living. However, one permanent con-tribution remained. The periodical published by this colony un-wittingly bequeathed its name, *The Social Gospel*, to this curious feature in American Protestantism.

Following the Civil War, the graduate students returning from Germany brought to all areas of American intellectual life the invigoration of German scholarship. In economics, they chal-lenged Adam Smith's laissez-faire. In philosophy, they were pro-ponents of German Idealism. In theology, they introduced the German historical study of the Bible.

The individualism of orthodox Christianity had been rooted in Biblicism. In most churches, the creedal orthodoxy of original Calvinism had been replaced, where orthodoxy remained at all, by a Bible orthodoxy somewhat like the Fundamentalist move-ment of our time. German historical criticism weakened the au-thority of the Bible, however, and thus contributed to the swing toward a collectivist interpretation of religion and life.

One of the first consequences of this new approach was the "discovery" that Jesus was primarily concerned with social re-form. A plethora of books were published after 1900 on the so-called "social teachings of Jesus."

Orello Cone, professor of Biblical Theology at St. Lawrence University, raised an unheeded voice against this misinterpreta-tion in *Rich and Poor in the New Testament* published in 1902. The more recent rise of the eschatological school of criticism has convinced many that the writings on the "social teachings of Jesus" represent the unhistorical tendency to make Jesus over into our own image.

TOP MAN OF THE SOCIAL GOSPEL

The saintly Baptist, Walter Rauschenbusch, greatest of the Christian Socialists, represents the pinnacle of the whole movement. The equal of his stature, the Social Gospel has not produced since.

Inheriting a deep religious spirit from a pietist background, he proved his complete sincerity by spending nine sacrificial years in a poverty stricken church in New York City. He later became professor of church history at Rochester Theological Seminary which furnished him with a vantage point from which he could speak to the nation.

Rauschenbusch attacked both competition and business monopoly, but advocated government monopoly with a naive confidence that politicians would be more altruistic. He assailed the profit motive as a thing of greed, but was essentially optimistic about human nature.

Albrecht Ritschl, a theological product of German Idealism, was a major influence in Rauschenbusch's thought. The Ritschlian emphasis upon the group (moral collectivism) was particularly vital to the Social Gospel. Salvation, for Ritschl, was not to be interpreted in terms of a future life, but in terms of service in a this-worldly kingdom of human goodness. In fact, Ritschl was convinced that God was not interested in saving the individual as such.

Although Washington Gladden arrived at Rauschenbusch's organic view of society by another avenue, Gladden differed in the emphasis placed upon the state which he thought to be the glue that holds society together. He said: "Let me say again that this conception of the state, that it is merely a police force, is, to my mind, a wholly erroneous conception; that the state is something far higher and more godlike than this and that if we could only invest it in our thought with its true divine character, we should need no other agency for the unification of society."

Rauschenbusch made a more religious approach. For him the redemption of society was to be found not in the state, but in the Kingdom of God which he called an "organizing energy" above and beyond both state and society. He felt the success of the Kingdom of God in saving the social order depended upon its pervasive presence within the social organism.

The phrase *social organism* marks a break in the American tradition. The early American had a contract theory of government derived from the Covenant Theology before John Locke had propounded the same. In a vague way, Americans had generalized this to explain society, and, in most cases, church organization. The organic view of the Social Gospel was a significant departure. Paul's analogy of the church as the "body of Christ" was used to justify the "organism of society," as a concept. But to apply Paul's analogy of the mystical, invisible church to the visible, organized church, or to the Kingdom of God, or worst of all, to secular society does injustice to Paul and results in utter confusion of thought.

The background of Rauschenbusch's *organism of society* was the Kantian Idealism of which Ritschl was an exponent. According to Kant, the state was an entity separate and distinct from the people who compose it. Rauschenbusch never carried his analogy that far, but this concept lurks in the background of Social Gospel thought.

LEGAL VERSUS MORAL PERSUASION

The humanistic trend of the Social Gospel from God to man, and the collectivist trend from the individual to the group, would not have been as alarming if this shift had not been accompanied by an eagerness to use political coercion to achieve what was thought to be the will of God. For instance, these social gospelers proposed that the majority should take property from the minority by using the power of government. This was to be an application of the "teachings of Jesus" and of the "law of love."

This passion to push people into the Kingdom of God is not novel in the history of Christianity. In fact, the state-church tradition has always had a weakness for legislating righteousness. However, the Separatist-Pietist tradition, which has constituted a major portion of American Protestantism, has preferred moral persuasion until it, too, became infected with the zeal of the Social Gospel.

NO MORAL ABSOLUTES

The Separatist-Pietist instinct bet its life on God and the moral order. It did not consider the moral universe in need of the assistance of the United States government. Unfortunately, however, faith in a moral universe sagged in the twentieth century. "Enlightened" Protestants no longer assumed that a moral order was written into the nature of things. Pragmatism invaded ethics. Some bluntly denied the existence of moral absolutes.

An historical criticism, not yet sufficiently historical, had not only made Jesus over into its own image, but had also "discovered" that the Ten Commandments were written to protect the "haves" against the "have-nots." Thus, "Thou shalt not steal" did not carry the weight in the twentieth century pulpit that it had in the nineteenth century. With this weakening of moral absolutes, the stage was set for the Social Gospel to come into its own.

Official denominational organizations devoted to the Social Gospel began springing up like mushrooms in the spring. The Presbyterian Department of Church and Labor of the Board of Home Missions was the first in America. In 1901, the National Council of the Congregational Churches founded a Labor Committee. The Methodist Episcopal Church (North) organized the Federation for Social Service in 1907. The following year this church adopted its famous Social Creed, the first of its kind to be adopted by any denomination.

This same year, thirty-three denominations founded the Federal Council of Churches of Christ in America which immediately adopted a Social Creed similar to that adopted by the Methodists.

The year 1908 also saw the Northern Baptist Convention pass a resolution urging the ministry and churches "to emphasize the social significance of the Gospel," but it was not until 1913 that the American Baptist Publication Society created a "Department of Social Service and Brotherhood."

By 1912, eleven denominations had pledged themselves to carry out social service programs. That same year, the interdenominational "Men and Religion Forward Movement," advocating government ownership of land, mines, water supply, etc., tried to unite the Social Gospel with the preaching enthusiasm of the old time religion.

The years after World War I brought a reaction against socialism. By 1924, the organized Christian Socialism that had flowered in numerous nondenominational "fellowships" dwindled to one – The Church League for Industrial Democracy.

The prosperity of the twenties made the emotional climate unfavorable for a message of class conflict, so the social gospelers shifted their emphasis to international and interracial problems. A bevy of peace organizations appeared in Protestant churches. In fact, President Wilson's League of Nations was described by the Federal Council of Churches as "an international manifestation of the Kingdom of God."

THE FERTILE DEPRESSION YEARS

During the depression, a reawakened Social Gospel found the time ripe for its message of sanctified covetousness. A questionnaire response from a large group of clergymen in 1934 indicated overwhelming bias against capitalism. The preference was for a "cooperative commonwealth" in which the service motive (rather than a profit incentive) would be predominant in individual life.

That same year, the Congregational-Christian churches established a Council for Social Action after passing a resolution to work toward:

> "The abolition of the system responsible for these destructive elements in our common life, by eliminating the system's incentives and habits, the legal forms which sustain it, and the moral ideals which justify it. The inauguration of a genuinely cooperative social economy democratically planned to adjust production to consumption requirements, to modify or eliminate private ownership of the means of production or distribution wherever such ownership interferes with the social good."

The Social Gospel as it developed in American Protestantism was not an application of the teachings of Jesus. It has been challenged to produce its intellectual and ethical credentials – and it has none.

REVEREND IRVING E. HOWARD

The
LIBERTARIAN
THEOLOGY
Of
FREEDOM

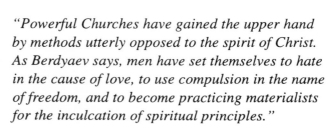

*"Powerful Churches have gained the upper hand
by methods utterly opposed to the spirit of Christ.
As Berdyaev says, men have set themselves to hate
in the cause of love, to use compulsion in the name
of freedom, and to become practicing materialists
for the inculcation of spiritual principles."*

– DEAN WILLIAM R. INGE
ST. PAUL'S CATHEDRAL, LONDON

CHAPTER ONE

THE ISSUES: A DEBATE

REV. JOHN C. BENNETT
Dean of the faculty and professor of Christian theology and ethics at Union Theological Seminary, NYC.*

REV. EDMUND A. OPITZ
A former Congregational parish minister, a former Director of Spiritual Mobilization. Staff member of the Foundation for Economic Education, Irvington, NY.*

Dear Mr. Bennett:

Your speech, *A Christian View of the State*, has been received and read with great interest. With many of your observations I find myself in agreement, but elsewhere I dissent vigorously. For example, even though you perceive that the state is the social apparatus of compulsion, you seem to say that there is nothing in Christian philosophy to tell us how that power ought to be limited.

I feel free to take exception to this position and others because, as I recall my seminary classes under you, they were occasions of mental adventure. You were not one to demand an echo of your own ideas from your students – you allowed us plenty of latitude. Although you may now feel that one with my convictions has taken exceptional liberties with that latitude, I like to

---

*As of 1956

think of the old observation that a teacher should take no credit for himself if a student resembles him overmuch.

Even while in seminary, the pronouncements on society which had issued from the various church councils, such as Oxford and Lambeth, and the social gospel idea itself, encountered a resistance in my thought. This obstruction was a way of thinking induced in large measure by the occasional essays of Albert Jay Nock in various journals. These essays led me to Nock's books and to other books mentioned in their pages. I found myself on the outskirts of a large and impressive body of thought. The more I got into it, the less was I able to stomach the prevailing mode of social thought among theologians and intellectuals. Their hankering after a planned economy, or a welfare state, or socialism, or a mixed economy, had little attraction for me. The remedy they urged, it seemed to me, was nothing but an articulate form of the disease: government force against persons to cure the evils caused by prior political intervention.

THERE ARE TWO SIDES

It has not been easy, during the past fifteen years – or perhaps for a much longer period – for a student going through college or seminary to escape being inoculated with a one-sided point of view. In this view, the instrumentality of government is regarded as a proper and efficient means to accomplish the end of general prosperity and security for individuals against the uncertainties of modern life. It is not so much that the social gospel or the welfare state idea is rammed down the student's throat, as that he is never adequately exposed to a radically different philosophy. The student gets by inference, if not more directly, the notion that a genuine concern for his fellows and for the good of society must lead a man to embrace the progressive extension of the functions and controls of government. Resistance to this idea is attributed to selfishness, or habit, or "the cultural lag," or to some unlovely general term like "reaction."

That there is another point of view relative to the role of the person vis-a-vis society and government, that it has long roots in the past and an impressive literature, and that it has a strong moral and intellectual case, is not part of the understanding which a student would be likely to gain from his formal education during the past decade or two. This other point of view is based on classic liberalism, as modified and developed by thinkers of the present century.

When one sees a caricature of this philosophy kicked around, and the real thing never mentioned, the first thought is that knowledge of it is deliberately kept from students. Experience has taught me otherwise. After perusing the books of the social gospellers and the welfarestaters, and after conversations with you and with men professionally engaged in one or the other of the various church councils for social action, I am forced to conclude that the reason why the libertarian case is not taught in seminaries is that the case is not known in theological circles! Neither is it a fashionable mode of thought among our intelligentsia; the climate of opinion is unfavorable to it. There are reasons for this state of affairs, and I hope we may sometime have occasion to explore them together.

THE POWER TO KILL

You say in the speech already referred to, "The state must have power; it must have the final power in the last resort to compel obedience." This is, I believe, a correct apprehension, and one that is held by virtually every political theorist – whatever else the state is, it is society's apparatus of coercion. You repeat this idea several times, as, for instance, "the state has ultimate power;" "the state cannot be a pacifistic institution;" "the state has a tremendous capacity for control;" and "the state has the power even to take life." When we speak of political power, we mean the legal warrant of those who exercise that power to interfere with willed action; to interpose by violence or the threat of violence between a man's will and conscience and the conduct these would enjoin on him. One does not employ political power, i.e., violence or the threat of violence, to make men act as they would act without it. For the kind of conduct men engage in normally and naturally, or can be educated or induced to engage in, political power is not needed. It is only where persuasion is ineffective that force is needed, and this force is exercised by society's agency of power, the state.

Once it is perceived that the distinctive feature of the agency of government is its possession of a virtual monopoly of the means of committing violence, then the problem facing all non-totalitarians is to find a principle by which government may be limited. Unless we embrace the philosophy that government is to engineer every area and relationship of life, we are faced with the problem of deciding what limitations shall be placed on it if it is to render service to society and not destroy society.

The business of society is peace; the business of government is violence. So, the question is: What service can violence render to peace? The libertarian answer is that violence can serve peace only by restraining peacebreakers.

NO CHRISTIAN JUDGMENT?

You say in your speech, "There is no Christian judgment as to where state power should end and various forms of private initiative should begin. This is an area where there must always be a great deal of experiment . . ." When you speak of "state power," you understand that it must be, as you say, "the final power in the last resort to compel obedience . . . the power to take even life." Are you saying that there is no Christian judgment as to the bounds which ought to limit the agency which has the power to compel obedience and to take life? The notion is so wild that I wouldn't accuse even a theologian of holding it except that one comes across similar expressions in your other writings.

Furthermore, there is a school of thought in theological circles close to you which appears to believe the same thing. They talk, as you do, of the state standing "under the sovereignty and the judgment of God." Then, having confidence that the Deity will take care of the ultimate outcome, they feel free to substitute the imperatives of the modern state for principles as a guide to conduct. They engage in "Realpolitik," in the experimental, piecemeal approach to social problems. Is there, then, no unique insight that religion can contribute to the understanding of social problems?

There is a lot of room here for further exploration, and I am hoping that you will feel inclined to enter upon it.

EDMUND A. OPITZ

Dear Mr. Opitz:

I appreciate the courtesy of your letter. Our presuppositions are so different that argument does not get very far. There may be some value in reflecting on the fact that I have no expectation of changing your thought and that you probably feel the same about me. Why should we have these stalemates so often in the discussion of controversial social issues? The following considerations may clear up a few misunderstandings.

THE STATE SHOULD BE LIMITED

1. You give quite a wrong impression of my thought when you suggest that I am not interested in the limiting of the state. I did say that there is no universal Christian law which can determine for us in advance exactly at what points the power and the functions of the state should be limited. When new situations arise it is often necessary for the state to assume new functions but within each situation these functions should be so defined as to protect the freedom of non-political associations and of individuals.

Basic to my thought is the emphasis on the distinction between the state and the community. The community includes many types of association and the swamping of the life of all other associations by the state is one of the greatest, perhaps the greatest, evil of our age. I am as much against the totalitarian state as you are.

The state should be limited by its own law which protects the freedom of minorities, of individuals, of many kinds of association. The state should be limited by the recognition on the part of the citizens that there is a law above the state and above the national community as well. The state should be limited by a pluralistic structure within the state itself, with division of powers, the independence of the judiciary, the recognition that functions should be distributed between various regional political units.

I wish that there were a universal formula that would enable us to know in detail what all of these forms of limitation should mean in practice but I believe that we have to work here experimentally rather than dogmatically to secure the best combination of institutions to fit the circumstances.

2. It is very misleading to speak as though coercion and violence were the essence of the state. It is quite true that the state is the only institution or association in the community that has the authority to coerce its members. There is a dark and forbidding element in this right of the state to exercise coercion even to the point of holding the power of life and death. But in order to preserve public order this authority must exist somewhere in the community. It is far from being the essence of the state.

The state exists to serve the purposes of the community, or what you call society. Many of these purposes do not involve the use of coercion. The better the state is and the healthier the community which it serves, the more the actions of the state will be based on consent. The life of the state is complicated by the necessity of providing for national defense. I hate this as much as you do. I see no way of dodging the responsibility.

WHAT IS THE ESSENTIAL ELEMENT?

At the opposite end there is the function of the state in providing educational opportunity for all children. This is primarily a constructive function that has little to do with coercion. The school system does depend on the collection of taxes, taxes which are collected in large measure because people are willing to pay them. Yet, there is a marginal element of coercion here because people would not be willing to pay if they believed that a considerable number would succeed in evading this obligation. So, there is coercion in the fulfillment of this constructive function of the state, but it is not the essential element in the school system.

I have tried to make clear that coercion is one distinctive mark of the state but that it is far from being the essence of the state. The healthier the state the smaller the part that coercion plays in its life.

THE MAIN ISSUE

3. I think that the chief difference between us is that you regard the state as the chief enemy of freedom in all situations whereas I believe that the state may be an instrument of freedom for its citizens. There are very important enemies of freedom with which the state alone can clear effectively.

One of them is the kind of coercion that results from the blind working of economic processes – the working of the business cycle. The increase of the functions of the state which you dislike most came as a result of the depression. The state in seeking to prevent a depression will have to assume some functions that it did not have in an earlier period but in doing so it will deliver millions of its citizens from the tyranny of circumstances that are beyond their control as individuals.

One aspect of this assumption by the state of some new powers to deal with new problems is that only so will it be possible to prevent the development of totalitarian movements in countries that are now free. Totalitarianism has not developed through the gradual expansion of the functions of the state to meet new problems. It has come out of the catastrophes that are the result of the failure of weak states to deal adequately with the problems of the people.

You and the group which you represent are pursuing a policy which will indirectly serve the very movements which you detest. You with your conception of the ineffective state are doing what you can to create a vacuum into which the advocates of totalitarianism may move.

It will require very great wisdom which is free from the dogmas of the right or the left to enable our country to steer a course in the next period that will use the state to help people preserve freedom from the tyranny of circumstances and from the tyranny of private centers of economic power without over-extending the activity of the state, especially without over-centralizing it.

I see those dangers as you do, but you seem to be blind to the opposite dangers which beset a society caught in crises with which the state is unable to deal because it lacks the authority and the appropriate instruments.

JOHN C. BENNETT

Dear Mr. Bennett:

In your gracious and helpful letter, you put your finger on several points at which the issues come into focus. This is most helpful, as it induces each of us to produce a more precise formulation of his views.

You have numbered three sections of your letter and I shall take them up in turn.

1. I know that you are not an absolutist and are concerned to limit the state. But certain questions were raised in my mind as to whether or not your thought gave evidence of any norms by which the state might be limited on principle. In my previous letter I questioned your relinquishment of *a priori* principles for judging what is and what is not within the competence of the state.

You list devices for limitation; and there I am all with you, but then you confirm my original doubts by saying, "We have to work here experimentally rather than dogmatically." This is not as explicit as one might wish, but it reads as though you are endorsing the prevailing view in these matters, that the moral principles by which individuals are judged do not apply when individuals act on behalf of government.

This is bluntly put in the book which you recommended in your speech as the best in the field, *Christianity and the State*, by William Temple. The author quotes the saying "What is morally wrong cannot be politically right," and comments "This maxim is usually intended, by those who make use of it, to declare that it cannot be right for the state to do what it would be wrong for an individual to do; and this is completely untrue." In short, the state is beyond the human judgments of good and evil which are relevant to individuals.

THE RIGHT OF SELF DEFENSE

I would take sharp issue with this point of view, which I gather is, or is close to, your own understanding of the matter. The reasoning behind the philosophy which holds that there are *a priori* moral principles which are relevant to politics runs somewhat as follows: If the individual has any inherent, God-given right to be on this earth at all, then he has the corollary right to defend his life. This is true of all men equally. They are within their moral rights to use force if need be to defend themselves against violence initiated against them.

If men individually have this moral right, they may severally delegate it provisionally to an agent. This agent, government, has the moral right to use force only as the delegating individuals have a right; namely, defensively to neutralize force. This accords with the basic principle that no man has a right to impose his will on another, and with its corollary that every person has a right to resist the imposition of an alien will over his own.

2. The true prototype of government is the constable, a man whose specialized occupation is to perform the necessary and social function of defense for members of society. Government is the social apparatus of coercion and compulsion. A law is not a mere suggestion; it has a penalty provision as a rider. There is no

need to pass a law to make people do what they do naturally or can easily be persuaded to do.

Every law supersedes the wills of some individuals, forcing them to do what their own will and conscience would not lead them to do; or, conversely, restrains them from doing what they want to do or think they ought to do. It is morally right to use legal force to frustrate criminal action for the protection of peaceful citizens. But the use of legal force against peaceful citizens is something else again. It impairs the moral principle which should guide political action.

There are two groups of men who tend to be unaware of the coercive nature of political action; those in the apparatus who actually carry out the compulsion, and those who, like yourself, advocate the extension of government functions, regulations, and controls.

When you advocate that a given social end be accomplished by means of government action, the construction of housing, say, you will persuade a few people. You would not, however, persuade people like myself who would regard your scheme as morally and economically unsound. Even though you could not persuade me, you could, if you succeeded in capturing the machinery of government for your purpose, force me to go along with you. I would be legally deprived of my property to further your scheme. If I decided to cast prudence aside and stand by my principles to the bitter end, I would be the victim of physical violence by agents of the state, and might even be killed resisting the officers who came to attach my property.

HELPING SOME BY HURTING OTHERS

This is not what you advocate, but it is the end product of your advocacy. If you are opposed to this end-product, you should desist from advocating the course of political action which produces it.

The sincere intention of the collectivist or the planner is to help people. But he chooses to help people through political action, which when spelled out means helping some people by hurting others. This injury to people can be made legal, and if there are only pragmatic and experimental sanctions for political activity, then I have nothing more to say. But if, as I believe, there are *a priori* moral principles by which political action is judged, then there is a real issue here.

3. Government is an instrument of freedom when it secures each person in his rights. To carry out this function, it may have to use coercion on individuals guilty of injuring other people.

You talk of another kind of coercion, that resulting "from the blind working of economic processes – the working of the business cycle." You use this phrase as if it is self-evident that men are put upon their mettle to consciously direct these processes by political action. One might speak about the blind working of the digestive processes, but when he does he recognizes that this means they are in good shape.

What you speak of as "the blind working of economic processes" is really the resultant of millions of individuals making voluntary decisions as to how they will dispose their limited energy so as to maximize their material and spiritual satisfactions. A planner can deprive them of this power of choice only by using force on them. His seizure of power brings economic chaos, but that is not all. Power ministers to human pride and brings spiritual disaster.

TYRANNY OF POWER

In the economic field, the only thing political power can do is grant privileges; that is to say, it can confer advantages on some at the expense of others. This has always and everywhere been a feature of political action.

You speak of "the tyranny of private centers of economic power." Examine anything you regard as a private center of economic power and you will find it always rests upon the prior grant of political privilege, a tariff, for instance, or a subsidy. Or else it represents the failure of government to enforce laws against predation. So long as there is political interference in the marketplace, which you advocate, there will be this kind of injustice and the resulting economic dislocations.

Your recommendation for fighting totalitarianism is to accept a little of its philosophy. I don't know what you intend to mean by the phrase "ineffective state," but I have some idea of what you mean by an effective one. An "effective state," in your view, is one which throws a vast network of regulations over economic activities, such as housing, insurance, medical care, electrical power, and so on. The libertarian does not want even an "ineffective state" in these realms, he wants the state out of these realms altogether. In these areas government cannot positively intervene without being an instrument of injustice. The libertarian does not want a weak government. He wants a government sufficiently virile and alert to perform adequately the functions within its competence.

THE PLANNED ECONOMY

The collectivist or planned economy philosophy has a grave defect. It tends towards a fixation, at the level of comprehension in social affairs men have now attained. It gives legal sanction to practices which trouble the sensitive conscience, and it places legal obstacles in the path of the gifted innovator. The libertarian philosophy, on the other hand, is open-ended toward life. It is so keenly aware of human limitations and pretensions to finality that it declares: No man has a right to impose his will on another.

The point of view that government should accept extended and accelerated functions in modern society, working experimentally and pragmatically, means that people will be politically directed and controlled in ever-widening areas of their lives. The logical end of such a scheme is a society in which whatever is not forbidden is compulsory. Practically, of course, it is recognized that things will stop short of this impossible ideal. But no matter the point at which an experimental equilibrium is reached, the individual is confronted with a considerable network of laws which severely narrow his choice of alternatives.

When government intervenes in the peaceful activities of its citizens, the range of human choice is limited. Thinking and action on a problem tend to stabilize around the government's provisional solution. Alternative means of accomplishing similar ends are penalized. Research on alternative solutions tends to dry up.

The libertarian philosophy aims to give every person full scope for the exercise of his faculties by allowing him the complete range of alternatives from which to choose. In order to secure this freedom for every person, one condition is laid down: No man has a right to impair the freedom of another. If a man, out of the wide range of alternative choices, elects to injure another, the law rightfully comes into play. It is morally right to use the coercive apparatus of government to defend each person in his life and possessions against the murderer, the thief, the libeller, the fraud. Men are free to make criminal choices, but in justice to other men, criminals must face the consequences of their actions.

A peaceful society is the equilibrium achieved under a system of the division of labor, the marketplace, the free exchange of goods, services, and ideas. This equilibrium is constantly threatened by private acts of initiated violence on the part of those who cannot or will not abide by the rules – and by government itself when it perverts its true function. The true function of government is to defend individuals by neutralizing this private violence with a display of whatever legal violence may be necessary. Government curbs the peacebreakers so that the peaceful business of society can go on, and in this action conforms to the moral norms which we recognize as binding upon individuals.

The issues of the modern world come down to a clash of principles. The appeal and apparent strength of the totalitarian philosophy is mainly in its bold logic. Accept its basic assumptions about the nature of man and society, and its conclusions about government follow in order.

I don't think men can confront it adequately unless they have a set of contrary principles and are willing to stand by the logic implicit in them. Those principles need further elucidation and the logic needs criticism, and I am grateful to you for the stimulus your comments will provide for men of an inquiring mind to sift these matters again.

EDMUND A. OPITZ

Dear Mr. Opitz:

I shall begin my answer by trying to clear up one apparent misunderstanding and then I shall deal with several major issues which divide us so completely that in our thinking about society we seem to live in two quite different worlds.

The misunderstanding has to do with your discussion of *a priori principles*. You assume that my experimental attitude toward the discovery of the precise limits of the state indicates that moral principles may apply to individuals in private life, but not to the policies of governments. I believe that the difficulty lies not in the absence of permanent and relevant moral principles, but in the fact that on most concrete issues in life we find that there is tension between the very principles by which we must act.

The most common tensions are between justice and freedom or order and freedom. Over and above all of the particular principles which should guide the actions of the Christian is the commandment of love for the neighbor, for all neighbors. The complexity of our moral decisions comes in part from the fact that there are conflicts between the interests and sometimes the real needs of our various neighbors. So most Christian decisions have to be made within very complex and rapidly changing situations with no *a priori* principle to settle for us exactly how we are to relate those competing principles and interests to each other at a moment of decision.

I do not believe for a minute that "the state is beyond the human judgments of good or evil which are relevant to individuals." It is true that the state has functions which are different from the functions of individuals. It should perform those functions for the sake of moral ends but the complexity of the conflict between values and interests is greater in the case of the state than it is in the case of the individual. The individual citizen who helps to make decisions about state policy, or the statesman who tries to implement policy, if he is a Christian, will be guided ultimately by a concern for the welfare and dignity of all of the people affected.

Motives controlled by this caring for all neighbors affected, humility before God which keeps us from allowing any *idea* of a social system or a social goal to become absolute or frozen, and continued sensitivity to the needs and interests of all the others who are involved – these are the Christian moral resources rather than *a priori* principles which are so precise that we can deduce concrete decisions from them in each situation.

Now, as to the issues which seem to divide us most deeply:

1. I fail to see that you have much place for the community or society as having value in itself. You deal with individuals who form states in self-defense but you have very little to say about the living community as such. Paul's words about our being "members one of another" applies to the church in the context of the epistle, but in a less complete way it applies to the community at large to which we all belong. The actual interdependence of men in community is obvious enough, but I have in mind something more: the possibility of realizing common values in society. A society is a better society, for example, if it is not divided into the very rich and the very poor, if there are no families within it who lack a certain minimum of protection against the hazards of unemployment, sickness and old age.

There is a *common good* which can only be obtained by common action. The state is in many cases the most useful instrument of common action. It should never become an end in itself and the common action which it makes possible should always be under moral criticism. Coercion of individuals who are unwilling to be taxed in order to make possible this common good may have its evil aspects, but it seems to me that you exaggerate it out of all proportion and that you never weigh it realistically against coercion by circumstances, which is often a far greater human burden. Moreover, I think that you do not take account of the fact that, when some forms of this common good are embodied in actual institutions and social habits, the vast majority of those who at first see only the fact that they are coerced come to recognize the common good for what it is and accept it as just.

2. Just as you seem to me to fail to emphasize society and the common good, also you seem to me to fail to emphasize the corporate, large scale threats both to the common good and to the welfare of individuals. Modern life is so complicated that its problems cannot be solved by many individuals acting independently. You apparently believe that the *laissez-faire* conception of economic life is still relevant and that individual decisions, freed from all interference by the state, can be counted on to assure a stable economy and a just society. I believe that you are consistent in this and that you would be as hard on the use of the state by business groups to obtain special privileges such as tariffs for themselves as you are on those who argue for a measure of economic planning. I believe that you are as much opposed in principle to private monopoly as to state intervention. Perhaps there would be much to be said for your position if we could return to a very simple individualistic economy with no vast enterprises and with very small units of interdependence. Actually you allow that picture of a simple economy to which it is now impossible to return, to obstruct the kind of action that is necessary to prevent disaster in the only economy which we are likely to have.

Take the one most obvious problem – the prevention of large scale and long continued unemployment when the defense spending begins to taper off. Do you believe that we can prevent a serious depression with socially disastrous unemployment if the nation as a whole fails to use government to devise corrective policies? If we were dealing with impersonal counters and not with people we might say: "let the deflation and the unemployment come until we get stability on a quite different level." But that is to ignore the human consequences of policy. The state will have to act with boldness and imagination to coordinate the efforts of private enterprise and to supplement private with public enterprise. For you to invoke *a priori* principles to inhibit such activity by the state is to assume responsibility for the immediate suffering which would result, and for the political and social consequences which are likely to follow.

I believe that we have a chance in this country to preserve large areas of private enterprise but there is one condition that must be met: there must be sufficient cooperation between government and the various elements in the economy to prevent socially disastrous inflation or deflation. If we fail at this point, the alternative to such a mixed economy is not your program of decentralization and of complete individualism but rather a state of tyrannical collectivism.

3. There is a basic difference of emphasis between us in connection with the question: with whose freedom are we most concerned? You seem to put all of your emphasis on the freedom of those who already have well established rights and privileges in society, who already have property or private sources of security. Your whole program neglects the people who are always in the vast majority and who have not yet won such a position of privilege or security. You may think that organized labor is catching up in this respect but this is a very recent development and it is doubtful if the gains of labor would survive a long depression without help from the state. The state often is able to defend the

weak against the strong. You cannot appeal to an earlier and purer capitalism in which this function of the state was not necessary. The past century has seen the very slow correction of the horrible exploitation and injustice of capitalism by the use of democratic processes. Karl Marx believed that this was impossible for he thought that democracy was a mere facade, but he was proven wrong and as a result we are developing in this country a real alternative to Marxist collectivism.

Central in this development is the opening up of opportunities for all children so that, as far as possible, they may have access to the kind of education and medical care and other advantages which will enable them to develop according to their capacities. There is still much more to be done along this line in this country. If you believe in equal opportunity for all, it is essential to do what can be done to counteract the inequality of opportunity for so many children resulting from the poverty of their parents.

PRIVATE CHARITY NOT ADEQUATE

This extension of opportunities, of rights and of freedom should not be left to private charity. One reason is that private charity is not adequate for the size of the problem. To me a more important reason is that this extension of opportunities should be regarded as a matter of justice. Christian generosity often shows itself best in the willingness to be taxed or to cooperate in the interests of justice. You may say that this is merely a case of "robbing Peter to pay Paul." But Peter's wealth is itself the product of a complicated social process to which the community as a whole contributes. The community has a responsibility to weigh many values and interests here and it must give great weight to the claims of Paul who, as a child, should have opportunities that are as good as those of Peter's child. If our American experience means anything it is doubtful if Peter will either suffer personally or lose his incentive.

Children have rights before they earn anything. But any citizen who works should be regarded as having rights which are the moral equivalent of the more familiar rights of property. In a complicated industrial society the rough and ready methods of determining who gets what are always in need of correction. Society owes it to itself that there be no large body of unemployed, but one can go beyond that and say that the individual worker wins, through years of work, something like a property right in his relation to his job. Even more obviously the man who has worked all of his life has a right to social security as one of the results of his labor.

In conclusion I shall bring together two criticisms of your position which underlie all that I say. The first is that you are so one-sided in your emphasis upon the economic freedom of those who are now strong enough to exercise it that you neglect many other values and needs to which the community must do justice. The second is that you look in only one direction for the threats to freedom. Freedom to be real must be accompanied by actual opportunity and to keep the door of opportunity open for all does require corporate action by the community through its instrument, the state. But even more important is the threat to freedom that comes when the problems of a complicated and dynamic economy go unsolved. It is in such a situation of popular frustration and despair that the promises of totalitarian shortcuts get their best hearing. Insofar as you are successful in preventing experiments in the solution of the real problems of our economy and of our people you and your movement will help to destroy freedom.

John C. Bennett

Dear Mr. Bennett:

Before we go further with our exchange of views by mail, there are some things I should like to say about your first two letters. The principal observation I want to make is that the very points which I think need further exploration and discussion are the premises you use for the cornerstones of your arguments. You seem to accept certain matters without question and assume that the only point at issue is one of eliciting proper conclusions.

When you note that my conclusions differ from your own, you seem to attribute the deviation to something more questionable than faulty logic.

I don't mean to say that the unexamined premises which I detect in your arguments are peculiar to you; they are widely held in this generation. The popular mind of any period is fettered in certain directions. It is as T. E. Hulme observed (in his *Speculations*) that "there are certain doctrines which for a particular period seem not doctrines, but inevitable categories of the human mind. Men do not look upon them merely as correct opinions, for they have become so much a part of the mind, and lie so far back, that they are never really conscious of them at all. They do not see them, but other things *through* them. It is these abstract ideas at the center, the things which they take for granted, that characterize a period."

POLITICAL MAGIC

The characteristic notion of our own time is that political action has an almost magical efficacy, a notion that seems to undergird your own thinking on these topics. I don't know how else to account for all the space you devote to showing the horrible results that must follow from holding rigorously to a philosophy of limited government. This is to beg the question, and also to prejudice it. For after your "demonstration" of the heinous consequences of our outmoded philosophy, the intelligent and responsible individual is led to infer that any organization built around such a philosophy must have some ulterior motive.

The concept of limited government which I hold will not, you say, even allow to government the powers it needs to prevent "large scale and long continued unemployment when defense spending begins to taper off." Because this philosophy will, you say, "obstruct the kind of action that is necessary to prevent disaster," you then charge that a depression would be a by-product of what we advocate.

I do not believe that political action is a panacea for institutional unemployment and other economic ills. A strongly held belief to the contrary characterized the thought in several modern totalitarian regimes, with consequences that each of us would deplore. The state is not a magic cure for economic ills; quite the contrary. In my first letter I suggested that the economic remedies peddled by the welfare state resolve themselves into an inequitable use of government coercion to cure the injustices resulting from earlier political intervention. In my second letter I came out more strongly and said that "in the economic field, the only thing political power can do is grant privileges; that is to say, it can confer advantages on some at the expense of others."

DEPRESSIONS TO ORDER

You chose to ignore these remarks; I shall therefore put the matter more bluntly. I am prepared to argue that a period of aggravated unemployment is not the result of alleged contradictions in the economic system, but the result of political intervention in economic affairs. Because this point of view is unpopular and may not be familiar to you, permit me to recommend one study which reveals the part played by government in causing economic dislocations. The book is Benjamin M. Anderson's massive treatise, "Economics and the Public Welfare, 1914-44." This book includes a blow by blow description of the political interventions which helped precipitate the stock market crash of 1929, and of the continuing interventions which kept our economy in the trough during the thirties. After you have looked into this book, it will not be quite so easy to assume as you do that there is a simple government remedy for unemployment and depression. For a broader and more theoretical treatment of this and allied questions, I recommend the various books of Ludwig von Mises.

I am amazed that you can speak with such assurance – at this late date – of the efficacy of political action in dealing with the problems of depression and institutional unemployment. I need only call your attention to the depression of 1937 and to the ten million unemployed in 1940, after billions of dollars had been spent in New Deal pump priming efforts, and after years of experimenting with one political remedy after another. Despite all this political intervention the decline in the curve for industrial production over an eight or nine month period in 1937-38 was the most violent of historical record in this country. Likewise, the break in the stock market was one of the sharpest in our history, working hardship on endowed institutions and on people dependent on unsalaried income.

The crisis of 1937 had a significant aftermath – the trend toward war gathered momentum galvanized by the desire to find another kind of political action more helpful than spending and controlling in staving off economic crises. Our unemployment problem was not "cured" until we entered the war, but I trust you do not have war in mind as a political remedy for economic ills.

You charge that our philosophy will not permit us to accept even those necessary government measures which would prevent "socially disastrous inflation or deflation." Perhaps both of us had better take another look at the mechanics of inflation, because so far as I have been able to find out, inflation is exclusively the result of a politically engineered dilution of our money supply. This is done directly by the government itself, or by agencies to whom government grants the privilege of controls over money and credit.[1] Inflation is not something government has to prevent; it is something government should itself stop doing. But perhaps you have an entirely different insight as to what brings about inflation. If so, I shall be interested in hearing about it.

BOGEYMAN TACTICS

You use bogeyman tactics when you proclaim, "You with your conception of the ineffective state are doing what you can to create a vacuum into which the advocates of totalitarianism may move." It seems to me somewhat hysterical to accuse someone of doing all he can to prepare the ground for totalitarianism, but apart from that, your use of the loaded phrase "the ineffective state" shows how far you are from having any comprehension of the role assigned to government in the thought of traditional liberalism and the modern libertarianism. I don't know of any libertarian who wants a "weak" government or an "ineffective" one. Whom do you have in mind?

You urge a point of view which is "free from the dogmas of the right or of the left." By inference, a label is pinned on our point of view; we spout "the dogmas of the right," and are thus opposed to the forward looking and humane middle. Labelling is much easier than analyzing, and the average man wants to avoid extremists and stick to the comfortable middle of the road. But if any objective thinking is to be done about social questions, it seems to me imperative to avoid the jargon and axioms of the press and radio. The terms in which most matters are popularly discussed are hardly the tools of careful thought. You can't analyze a cake of soap in the same language you use to sell it!

Your letters seem to have a theme song about like this: In contrast to the righteousness of the collectivist position in these matters, the libertarian philosophy – no matter what its intellectual pretensions – is a thinly disguised defense of things as they are. On several occasions you cannot quite contain yourself and the theme becomes explicit. We are charged with being callous toward human suffering which a benevolent government could prevent, and "indifferent to the human consequences of policy." You assail us with seeming "to put all of your emphasis on the freedom of those who already have well established rights and privileges in society." You accuse us of opposing any political move "to counteract the inequality of opportunity for so many children resulting from the poverty of their parents." Our strong partisanship, you say is evident in that we appear to be "one-sided in our emphasis upon the economic freedom of those who are strong enough to exercise it."

This is a serious charge, that the libertarian philosophy is little more than a front for the interests of the wealthy and the powerful. But the charge may also be a serious reflection on the person making it. Analyzing and criticising a philosophy is one thing; passing an adverse moral judgment on the persons holding it is quite another. Brooding over one's moral superiority to those who hold differing convictions is not conducive to the health of the soul.

In making these charges, your unexamined premises come into play once again. The question at issue is whether or not the general welfare is best served by political action which deprives some people of their belongings for the express purpose of distributing them politically to someone else.[2] In addition to the matter of the moral propriety of this kind of political action, it can be demonstrated, I think, that it leads to the economic impoverishment of the very people you say you want to help. If you want increased opportunity for underprivileged children as well as for everyone else, the use of political tools is, in my opinion, the wrong means to use to reach this goal.

There is some ambiguity in your classification, "those who already have well established rights and privileges in society." In my second letter I indicated my acceptance of the concept of natural rights; every person has an inherent, God-given right to live, and all that this implies. But it does not imply the right to live at the expense of someone else! I would understand by your usage of the phrase "well established rights," that you mean to imply an advantage at the expense of someone else, a privilege — the denial of natural rights. I cannot conceive of a situation of this sort except as it is maintained by the exercise of political

---

[2]For an extended treatment of the idea that political action is invariably coercive, see "The Lengthening Shadow of Government," by Edmund A. Opitz, The Foundation for Economic Education, Irvington, New York, 1954. (Editor's note)

power, or else as the result of a failure on the part of government to do its job of securing individuals in their rights. Can you name an instance of any person or groups possessing an advantage at the expense of someone else where government is not working actively on behalf of the exploiter – or at least passively by neglecting its proper duty of defending all men equally against invasions of their rights?

Basic to your thought in this area is the concept of vast majorities who cannot take care of themselves. They are too foolish, too weak, too gullible. You, and a few other souls who really care, feel the need to scurry around and garner the power for government to force somebody else to do something for these poor folk. Tolstoy made an observation that bears directly on your little crusade. He said, "People will do everything for the poor except get off their backs." This is the job for government in libertarian thought, to destroy parasitism by pulling people off their victim's backs. For this we need a government strong enough and just enough to do that job.

THE COMPETENCE OF GOVERNMENT

Perhaps this debate would be more helpful if we got down to particulars. Your position seems to be that the coercive power of government should be used to make some people pay for the "advantages" bestowed upon the "underprivileged." These political favors would be in the form of public housing, socialized medicine, easy money from the Reconstruction Finance Corporation, and so on. My position is that the efforts to cure or relieve these situations by political intervention result in a worsening of the situation even from the viewpoint of those for whom the intervention is advocated. For example, if low cost housing for the poor is your goal and public housing is your method, then I am prepared to argue that the method is not equipped to achieve that goal. It has the opposite result of the one intended; namely, fewer low cost housing units available for those who need them.

In brief, the political interventions which you advocate for the achievement of a variety of social goals will result, not in what you say you visualize but in the opposite. If the goal is better housing for all people, better medical care, better education, and a peaceful society, then positive political intervention for these purposes makes no sense. On the other hand, if the goal is the attainment of power over people, then intervention does make sense.

A discussion of the practical consequences to actual men and women resulting from political action leads into the question of the principles which should guide such action. I urged the simple proposition that the morality which is recognized as binding upon persons acting as private individuals, is also binding when those same individuals act on behalf of, or as the agency of, government. I do not mean to imply that this principle is simple in application; but that the meaning is fairly clear. It is what John Bright had in mind when he said, "The moral law was not written for individuals only, but for nations, and for nations as great as we are." Perhaps even more widespread than the belief in this concept, is the notion of a double standard of morality, one for people and another for politicians. A quotation from Frederick the Great comes to mind to illustrate this double standard, "I hope that posterity will distinguish the philosopher from the monarch in me, and the decent man from the politician."

You took this simple proposition and strove mightily with it through sizeable portions of your two letters, but you avoided giving a clear-cut answer. You tried to make it appear that I was arguing for a science of politics, such as has been attempted by a few theorists, which would in effect give the statesman a push button method of conducting his affairs; he would have at his elbow a ready calculator with all the answers he needs to cope with life's many contingencies. It is in your rephrasing of what I said that this straw man appears. Let me quote and italicize. You said that there is "no universal Christian law which can determine for us in advance *exactly*, at what points the power and functions of the state should be limited." You disavowed the ex-istence of "a *universal formula* that would enable us to know *in detail* what *all* these forms of limitation should mean in practice." You remarked that there are "no a priori principles which are so *precise* that we can deduce concrete decisions from them in *each* situation." If this playback is your rendering of what I said about a single moral code operative alike on the individual and on government, I am forced to insert a disclaimer and say that the one bears no resemblance to the other.

You raise yet another objection to the consideration of the moral principles which apply to the policies of governments. "I believe," you say, "that the difficulty lies not in the absence of permanent and relevant moral principles, but in the fact that on most concrete issues in life we find that there is tension between the very principles by which we must act." Do you mean to say that there is really tension and conflict between the "principles by which we must act?" Or is there apparent tension because of human ignorance and self will? Would you explain more fully your understanding of this point? In any case, this stricture is equally relevant (or irrelevant) to the moral problems which be-set the person in private action and in political action. If this is a problem for political morality it is equally a problem for interper-sonal morality. But you immediately use this stricture to argue against the idea that there are moral principles binding on politi-cal and personal action alike. You conclude this argument by speaking as if the effort to apply moral principles to politics is to allow an "idea of a social system or a social goal to become abso-lute or frozen." With respect to our understanding of the meaning of words, we do, as you say, "seem to live in two quite different worlds."

POLITICAL VIOLENCE

On yet another matter, you read into my remarks a meaning which is quite different from what I intended. I made the rather commonplace observation several times that when government acts, violence or the threat of violence lies behind its action. The political agency is society's apparatus of coercion, its social role is to secure the individual in his freedom. That is, government should endeavor to maintain a situation in which no man may supersede another man's will by subjecting it forcibly to his own. The forcible overriding of any man's will by an alien will must be sharply distinguished from two other situations with which it is often confused. If one man *induces* another to act as he wants him to act by persuasion or education, he does not supersede his will, he gains his consent – a fundamentally different thing. And again, there is a substantive difference between using violence to resist another's effort to subject your will to his, and the use of violence to impose your will on him. In the former instance, violence is used to neutralize or cancel out violence; while in the latter, the violence is initiated against another.

A society is free when its members resist the tendency to interfere by force with the lives of others. In this kind of a society, justice is established as each person is given his clue and no man has a politically conferred advantage over any other. The only desirable kind of equality exists, in that no man has the privilege of living at the expense of his neighbor. Social order is present to the extent which freedom, justice and equality prevail – and they prevail to the extent that initiated violence is minimized in deference to a prevailing moral code.

When the contrary view comes to prevail, with a lot of loose talk about the tensions between freedom and order, and freedom and justice, together with a belief that the establishment of social order rests upon political action, then we get that trend toward disintegration which the modern world exhibits. Social order cannot be established by political violence however legal, but it can be destroyed in a hurry by such violence.

I nowhere argued that coercion and violence are the "essence" of government, but this does not discourage you from insisting that it is "misleading to speak as though coercion and violence were the *essence* of the state," that "this authority . . . is far from being the *essence* of the state," and yet once more within the space of a few paragraphs, "coercion . . . is far from being the *essence* of the state." The political agency *in action* relies on violence or the threat of violence to carry through a policy. The permissive limits within which this agency acts are set by the mores of the community. Popular consent is given for the use of political coercion in certain directions and not in others. The critical factors here are: a popular understanding of what political action involves, and a set of values which sets limits to what shall be done to people by violence or the threat of violence.

Only Government Establishes Monopoly

In your first letter you shuddered at the effects of what you called "the tyranny of private centers of economic power." I countered by saying that such tyrannical centers do not exist except as a result of the political agency refraining from its proper function or engaging in improper ones. It would be helpful if you would name an example of what you regard as tyrannous economic power which does not rest on a political base of either overt action or negligent inaction. In your second letter you speak of a "private monopoly," which is a contradiction in terms, unless you use the word monopoly in a metaphorical sense to describe individual talents. No profitable monopoly is possible if there are competitors, and there will be competitors unless political interference suppresses them.

In your second letter you wrote as if I believed in "individual decisions, freed from all interference from the state." This is one more example of your failure to grasp the part assigned to the political agency in libertarian thought, which is grave neglect for a teacher who works in the special field of social thought. What is more, the point arose and was dealt with several times in the first two letters. An individual decision to injure another is rightly interfered with by the political agency. I remarked that the normal, peaceful business of society needs the political agency to restrain the peacebreakers. Government defends individuals by neutralizing private violence; the law rightfully comes into play when anyone invades the prerogatives of another. It is morally right to use legal force to frustrate criminal action for the protection of peaceful citizens. This principle is diametrically opposed to that which urges the use of legal force against peaceful citizens. Now it may be that – to you – these principles read like an advocacy of "individual decisions, freed from all interference by the state." They read quite otherwise to me.

You observe that modern life is so complex that "its problems cannot be solved by many individuals acting independently," and I quite agree with you. But social cooperation under the division of labor, a marvelously intricate affair of human collaboration, is hardly to be described accurately as simply "many individuals acting independently." The mutual actions of men in society, when uncoerced, helps all participants attain their own ends without injuring others. Social cooperation based on the marketplace puts a surplus of energy at the disposal of human beings which makes it possible for individual men and women to seek and find that fulfillment which each regards as his own destiny. The notion of men as an isolated anarch who has to have his talons lopped off before he can enjoy the fellowship of his own kind, is a fable – besides raising the question of who will do the lopping. Man lives and works in cooperation with his fellows because he is made for mutuality and community, and he discovers what the social situation is to his own advantage, materially and spiritually. To speak of man's original freedom which he must sacrifice in society for the sake of order; or to say, as you have on other occasions that "the individual should dedicate himself to the welfare of the group," is to use words that refer to no discoverable reality.

TO COERCE OR NOT

You admit that a certain amount of coercion must be practiced upon those persons who are reluctant to be taxed for the attainment of certain ends by means of political action. You believe that this coercion must be viewed in the light of a necessary evil, and I exaggerate it, you say, out of all proportion. Besides, I never "weigh it realistically against coercion by circumstances." Let us be perfectly clear about what it is you are here saying. First of all, you are saying that it is all right to override the wills of a few people – a recognized evil – in order that a good end may be accomplished. And anyway, some of those who are coerced frequently come to see the error of their recalcitrance, and in the light of the good results obtained, accept the matter as just. It would be a dubious ethical theory that could be erected on such reasoning as this. Let me quote from the late Archbishop Temple's great book *Nature, Man and God*, on the meaning of ethical good in a situation similar to this one. He says, ". . . it is better that thousands should die in tumults rather than that order should be preserved at the cost of injustice voluntarily done to one innocent man. For the suffering and death of the body does not involve deterioration of character; but that injustice should be inflicted on innocence is an outrage on the sanctity of personality, while voluntarily to inflict it is to repudiate that sanctity and the obligations which it imposes." (P. 194)

Secondly, you use the same word, "coercion," to convey two distinct meanings. In the first instance, "coercion" is used in the sense of some men subjecting other men to their wills. In the second instance, you speak of "coercion by circumstances." I don't know what you mean by this unless you mean those mandates of the naturale and the sacred order to which man must accommodate himself, and those contingencies with which he must cope. To confuse the necessities and imperatives of the human situation with the all-too-human vice of imposing one will on another by calling two such dis-similar things by the same word, "coercion," is to be guilty of what may well be termed The Fallacy of the Onomatopoetic Middle: Two things equal to the same sound are equal to each other!

You repeat the oft-used phase about a man acquiring "a property right in relation to his job." In this time of a general debasement of the language, property is one of the words that has suffered most. Many things called property are not property at all. The word has been personified, and some have talked about property having rights. Only human beings have rights, and they have a right to own, control, and dispose of the material things which their labor of mind and muscle has produced, and in addition, to the things they have acquired by exchange and as gifts. Contrary to what you say, there are not "rough and ready methods of determining who gets what;" there is a delicately articulated device called, for short, "the market." Actually, the market is the resultant of millions of voluntary choices made by men and women as they quest for the highest satisfactions of those things they value most. What each of these millions may call his own is what others voluntarily accede to him. The reluctance to play this game according to the rules derives from the fact that each of us tends to overvalue his own goods and services and undervalue those of others. We are not content with the valuation others place upon our goods and services, and we join the struggle to get at the machinery of the political agency, in the expectation that, having control of it, other men can then be forced to value our product at its "true" worth.

WHAT IS A JOB?

In relation to a job, we tend to believe that our wages are too low while others' prices are too high – and everybody believes exactly the same about us. What is commonly called a job, is the result of an opportunity created by the accumulation of from a few thousand to a hundred thousand dollars* in the form of machines and a place to use them. In the most recently constructed large steel mill, the investment per worker was one hundred thousand dollars – it cost that much for the equipment used to employ one man. In the twisted thinking of our time, the group of citizens which invests its savings and puts its property at the disposal of other men so that these men may labor more effectively, is not performing a service. The motives of the group are challenged and its membership is subject to a crossfire of laws. To urge, as you do, that a person who is allowed to use another's property acquires a "right" to it, can have only one result – to discourage those accumulations which create jobs and to fail to use that which has been accumulated. No man will allow another to use his property if he is going to lose it thereby. The tools and machines which have produced in this country an abundance by comparison with other countries in the world, will not be available to the next generation. It may be that the next generation will want to embrace voluntary poverty, but I'd feel better if it is left to them and the matter of poverty is not thrust upon them by us through the policies you advocate.

You may want to deny this result of your policies. "If our American experience means anything," you say, "it is doubtful if Peter (who is robbed to pay Paul) will either suffer personally or lose his incentive." Perhaps you should say, rather, that you have not bothered to look into the studies which present alarming evidence on this point. The best introduction I know of to this topic is a pamphlet by Dr. F. A. Harper entitled "Eating the Seed Corn" which I am enclosing.

There is one point at which I should like to get a clarification of your meaning. You say, "A society is a better society . . . if it is not divided into the very rich and the very poor." You place this in a context containing such airy phrases looking in vain for a

---

*In 1950 dollars.

referent as "a common good which can be reached only by common action," and "the living community as such." Despite any qualifications that may lie concealed in these phrases, I think it safe to say that I am as much opposed as you are to a society divided arbitrarily into the very rich and the very poor. But I don't know of any special breed of people who are easily classifiable as "the very poor." From my observations, I would say that most of the people who are thus labelled would do all right for themselves were they not the victims of predation of the legal variety.

SOAK THE POOR

Not only do you countenance this kind of predation, but you advocate it. For I cannot believe that you would represent political intervention merely as a simple procedure in which the rich are soaked to help the poor. People with small incomes pay a large part of the current costs of running the kind of political establishment you advocate. You have not suggested doing away with wealth differentials, so presumably the political intervention you want is to be exercised somewhat arbitrarily according to the way *you* think wealth ought to be distributed. Your thought seems to stress what other people ought to be forced to do, and I cannot deduce from it what immediate and voluntary steps you personally would take. Perhaps you would be disposed to enlarge on this point in some future letter.

If nothing else is clear from this exchange of letters, one thing at least does stand out; that what you criticize as the libertarian philosophy bears little relation to what I and others understand by that philosophy. These letters will have served a useful purpose if the widespread misunderstanding that surrounds these matters is removed to any degree. In any event, I think we now understand each other a little better.

I hope you have under advisement the suggestion I made earlier, that a small but representative group of men whose thinking is close to your own, meet with a group of representative libertarians, for several days of informal but earnest discussion. I am sure that nothing but good can come from such a meeting.

With every good wish.

EDMUND A. OPITZ

Dear Mr. Opitz:

I found your letter here when I returned from Europe toward the end of August. I find that we think and talk past each other so much that detailed argument becomes very difficult. I hope that you are publishing the letters so that other people can work on the problem. After the immediate pressures of the new term are over, we may be able to talk about the whole problem again.

Probably your proposal about a meeting of a group representing two approaches should be discussed by Christian Action. I will pass on your letter to our secretary, Mr. Gessert.

JOHN C. BENNETT

---------------◈---------------

*". . . those benevolent principles of Christianity,
which inculcate the natural freedom of mankind."*

— EDWARD GIBBON, ROMAN HISTORIAN

---------------◈---------------

Chapter Two

Roots Of American Liberty

It was once the unwritten rule in polite society that two topics have no place in civilized conversation: religion and politics. It was ill-bred to discuss religion; it was gauche to talk politics. But times have changed. We live in a different and more open age. Now we discuss religion for political reasons, and we talk politics for religious reasons! The Bishops issue a Letter; the highest dignitaries of the various denominations pronounce on matters of government and business. The people behind these proclamations represent only a tiny minority of the total church membership, but they presume to speak for everyone. What they say is, in effect, the Socialist Party platform in ecclesiastical drag.

The First Amendment to the Constitution forbids Congress to set up an official church; there was to be no "Church of the United States" as a branch of this country's government. Such an alliance between Church and State is what "establishment" means. An established church is a politico-ecclesiastical structure that receives support from tax monies, advances its program by political means, and penalizes dissent. Our Constitution renounces such arrangements *in toto*; the Founders wrote the First Amendment into the Constitution to prevent them.

This essay won the Amy Foundation Award for of $5,000 in 1991. It was published in *Freeman*, July, 1991 and was included in Reverend Opitz' book, *Religion: Foundation of the Free Society*, published by the Foundation for Economic Education. (Ed.)

The famed American jurist Joseph Story, who served on the Supreme Court from 1811 till 1845, and is noted for his great *Commentaries on the Constitution of the United States*, had this to say about the First Amendment: "The real object of the Amendment was, not to countenance, much less advance Mahommedanism, or Judaism, or infidelity, by prostrating Christianity; but to exclude all rivalry among Christian sects, and to prevent any *national* ecclesiastical establishment, which should give to an hierarchy the exclusive patronage of the national government."

The various theologies, doctrines, and creeds found in this country can thus be advanced by religious means only – by reason, persuasion, and example. Separation of Church and State means that government maintains a neutral stance toward our three biblically based religions – Catholicism, Judaism, and Protestantism, as well as toward the various denominations and splinter groups. These several religious bodies, then, have no alternative but to compete for converts in the marketplace of ideas. This is a good arrangement, good for both Church and State; it avoids the twin evils of a politicized religion and a divinized politics.

A CHRISTIAN NATION

It has often been observed that America is a Christian nation – around which observation several misunderstandings cluster. We are a Christian nation in the sense that our understanding of human nature and destiny, the purpose of individual life, our convictions about right and wrong, our norms, emerged out of the religion of Christendom – not out of Buddhism, Confucianism, or primitive animism. And it is a fact of history that our forebears whose religious convictions brought them to these shores in the seventeenth and eighteenth centuries sought to create in this new world a biblically based Christian commonwealth. But it was not to be a theocracy – of which the world had seen too many! It was to be a religious society, but one which incorporated a *secular* political order!

The reasoning ran something like this. The human person is forever; each man and woman lives in the here and now, and also in the hereafter. Here, we are pilgrims for three score years and ten, more or less. Life here is vitally important for it's a test run for life hereafter. Earth is the training ground for life eternal. Such training is the essence of religion, and it's much too important to be entrusted to any secular agency. But there is a role for government; government should maintain the peace of society and protect equal rights to life, liberty, and property. This maximizes liberty, and in a free social order men and women have maximum opportunity to order their souls aright.

Separating the sacred and the secular in this fashion is a new idea in world history. Secularize government and you deprive it of the perennial temptation of governments to offer salvation by political contrivances. By the same token, things sacred are privatized as free churches, where the spiritual concerns of men and women are advanced by spiritual means only.

So, when it is said that America is a Christian nation, the implication intended is poles apart from what is meant when it is observed, for example, that Iran is a Shiite nation. The Shiite sect of Islam is a branch of the government of Iran. Other religions are not tolerated. Deviations from doctrinal orthodoxy are forbidden. The government punishes infidels because Shiism is Iran's official, authorized church. From time to time government uses the sword to gain converts. The government of Iran is not neutral with respect to religion.

In the United States, it is mandated that the government maintain a level playing field, so to speak, "a free field and no favor," where freely choosing individuals find their different pathways to God while government merely keeps the peace. This is what is really meant by the phrase, "Separation of Church and State." This oft-quoted phrase is frequently misunderstood as suggesting that religion and politics are incompatible, and that we should keep religion out of politics.

If we think of "politics" as several candidates wheeling, dealing, and slugging it out in an election campaign, it's clear that religion doesn't have a significant role in such a situation. And if we think of "religion" in terms of a contemplative meditating and praying in his cell, it's obvious that politics is absent. But there is no coherent political philosophy apart from a foundation of religious axioms and premises.

RELIGION AND THE SOCIAL ORDER

Religion, at its fundamental level, offers a set of postulates about the universe and man's place therein, including a theory of human nature, its origin, its potentials, and its destination. Religion deals with the meaning and purpose of life, with man's chief good, and the meaning of right and wrong. Thus, religious axioms and premises provide the basic materials political philosophy works with. The political theorist must assume that men and women are thus and so, before he can figure out what sort of social and legal arrangements provide the fittest habitat for such creatures as we humans are. So, some religion lies at the base of every social order.

It is the religion of dialectical materialism that is the take-off point for the Marxian theory and practice of the total state. Hinduism is basic to the structures of Indian society. Western society, Christendom, was shaped and molded by Christianity. Incorporated into Western civilization were elements from the Bible, as well as ingredients from Greece and Rome. This composite was lived, worked over, and thought out for nearly 1,800 years by the peoples of Europe. And then something new emerged and began to take root in the New World; it was the recovery of that part of the Christian story needed to ransom society from despotism and erect the structures of a free society wherein men and women might enjoy their birthright of economic and political liberty.

A vision emerged of a society where men and women would be free to pursue their personal goals, unimpeded by the fetters of rank,

early Christian notion of equality before God . . . The debt of democracy to Christianity has always been under estimated . . . Long before Rousseau was ever heard of, or Locke or Hobbes, the fundamental principles of democracy were plainly stated in the New Testament, and elaborately expounded by the early fathers, including St. Augustine.

"Today, in all Christian countries, equality before the law is almost as axiomatic as equality before God. A statute providing one punishment for A and another for B, both being guilty of the same act, would be held unconstitutional every where, and not only unconstitutional, but also in plain contempt of common decency and the inalienable rights of man. The chief aim of most of our elaborate legal machinery is to give effect to that idea. It seeks to diminish and conceal the inequities that divide men in the general struggle for existence, and to bring them before the bar of justice as exact equals."

The freedom quest of Western man, as it has exhibited itself periodically over the past 20 centuries, is not a characteristic of man as such. It is a cultural trait, philosophically and religiously inspired. The basic religious vision of the West regards the planet earth as the creation of a good God who gives a man a soul and makes him responsible for its proper ordering; puts him on earth as a sort of junior partner with dominion over the earth; admonishes him to be fruitful and multiply; commands him to work; makes him a steward of the earth's scarce resources; holds him accountable for their economic use; and makes theft wrong because property is right. When this outlook comes to prevail, the groundwork is laid for a free and prosperous commonwealth such as we aspired to on this continent.

A CREATED BEING IN A CREATED WORLD

We gaze out upon the world around us and are struck by the preponderance of order, harmony, beauty, balance, intelligence, and economy in the way it works. The thought strikes us that the explanation of the world is not contained within the world itself, but is to be sought in a Source outside the world. The Bible simply declares that God created the world, and when He had finished He looked out upon the world He had created and called it good. The biblical world is not *Maya* – as Hinduism calls its world; it is not a mirage or an illusion. Nor is the world of nature holy; only God is holy. The created world, including the realm of nature, is "the school of hard knocks." The earth challenges us to understand its workings so that we might learn to use it responsibly to serve our purposes. Economics and the free enterprise system teach us how to use the planet's scarce resources providently, efficiently, and non-wastefully – in order to produce more of the things we need.

Man comes onto the world scene as a created being. As a created being, man is a work of divine art and not a mere happening; he possesses free will and the ability to order his own actions. As such, he is a responsible being. He's no mere chance excrescence tossed up haphazardly by physical and chemical forces, shaped by accidental variations in his environment. To the contrary, man is endowed with a portion of the divine creativity, giving him the power to dynamically transform himself, and his environment as well, according to his needs and his vision of what ought to be.

The other orders of creation – animals, birds, bees, fish, and so on – live by the dictates of their instincts. But our species has no such infallible inner guidelines as our fellow creatures possess; our guidelines are formulated in the moral code, as summed up in the Ten Commandments.

Ethical relativism is a popular attitude today; it is a wrong answer to such questions as: Is there a moral code? Are there moral laws? Let me summarize briefly the argument that our universe has a built-in moral order by showing that there is a striking parallel between the laws of physical nature and moral laws.

The laws of science translate into words the observed causal regularities in the world of physical nature, i.e., the realm of things which can be measured, weighed, and counted. This is one sector of reality. Reality also exhibits a moral dimension, where things are valued or disdained on a scale of ethics ranging from good to evil. Biological survival depends on conforming our actions to the laws of nature; ignorance is no excuse. Social survival, the enhancement of individual life in society, depends on willing obedience to the moral code that condemns murder, theft, false witness, and the rest. Transgressors lead us toward social decay and cultural disorder.

Your individual *physical* survival depends on several factors. If you want to go on living you need so many cubic feet of air per hour, or you suffocate. You need a minimum number of calories per day, or you starve. If you lack certain vitamins and minerals specific diseases will appear. There is a temperature range within which human life is possible: too low and you freeze, too high and you roast. These are some of the requirements you must meet for individual bodily survival. They are not statutory requirements, nor are they mere custom. They are laws of this physical universe, which one can deny only at his peril.

ESTABLISHING A MORAL ORDER

It is just as obvious that our survival as a community of men, women, and children depends on meeting certain *moral* requirements: a set of rules built into the nature of things which must be obeyed if we are to survive as a society – especially as a social order characterized by personal freedom, private property, and social cooperation under the division of labor.

Moses did not invent the Ten Commandments. Moses intuited certain features of this created world that tell us what we must do to survive as a human community, and he wrote out the code: Don't murder, don't steal, don't assault, don't bear false witness, don't covet. Similar codes may be found in every high culture.

It would be impossible to have *any* kind of a society where most people are constantly on the prowl for opportunities to murder, assault, lie, and steal. A good society is possible only if most people most of the time do not engage in criminal actions. A good society is one where most people most of the time tell the truth, keep their word, fulfill their contracts, don't covet their neighbor's goods, and occasionally lend a helping hand. No society will ever eliminate crime, but any society where more than a tiny fraction of the people exercises criminal tendencies is on the skids. To affirm a moral order is to say, in effect, that this universe has a deep prejudice against murder, a strong bias in favor of private property, and hates a lie.

The history of humankind in Western civilization was shaped and tempered by biblical ideas and values, and the attitudes inspired by these teachings. There was much backsliding, of course; but in the fullness of time scriptural ideas about freedom, private property, and the work ethic found expression in Western custom, law, government, and the economy – especially in our own nation. We prospered to the degree that we practiced the freedom we professed; we became ever more productive of goods and services. The general level of economic well-being rose to the point where many became rich enough so that biblical statements about the wealthy began to haunt the collective conscience.

The Bible does warn against the false gods of wealth and power, but it legitimizes the normal human desire for a modicum of economic well-being – which is not at all the same as *idolizing* wealth and/or power. As a matter of fact, the Bible gives anyone who seeks it out a general recipe for a free and prosperous commonwealth. It tells us that we are created with the capacity to choose; we are put on an earth which is the Lord's and given stewardship responsibilities over its resources. We are ordered to work, charged with rendering equal justice to all, and to love mercy. A people which puts these ideas into practice is bound to become better off than a people which ignores them. These commands laid the foundation for the economic well-being of Western society.

Western civilization, which used to be called "Christendom," did not prosper at the expense of the relatively poor Third World. This unhappy sector of the globe is poor because it is unproductive; and it is unproductive because its nations lack the institutions of freedom that enabled us to achieve prosperity.

During recent years a small library of books and study guides has poured off the presses of American church organizations (and from secular publishers as well) with titles something like "Rich Christians (or Americans) in a Hungry World." The allegation is that *our* prosperity is the cause of *their* poverty; in other words, the Third World has been made poor by the very same economic procedures – "capitalism" – that have made Western nations prosperous! Therefore – the argument runs – our earnings should be taxed away from us and our goods should be handed over to Third World countries – as a matter of social justice! The false premise is that the wealth we have labored to produce has been gained at their expense. Sending them our goods, then, is but to restore to the Third World what rightfully belongs to it! What perverse ignorance of the way the world works!

Nations of the West were founded on biblical principles of justice, freedom, and a work ethic, which led naturally to a rise in the general level of prosperity. Our wealth could not have come from the impoverished Third World where there was a scarcity of goods. We prospered because of our productivity; we became productive because we were freer than any other nation. Freedom in a society enables people to produce more, consume more, enjoy more; and also to give away more – as we have done – to the needy in this land and in lands all over the world. The world has never before witnessed international philanthropy on such a scale.

No one has denied Third World nations access to the philosophical and religious credo which has inspired the American practices that make for economic and social well-being. Few nations have done more to make the literature of liberty available to all who wish it than American missionaries, educators, philanthropists, and technicians. But there is something in the creeds of Third World countries that hinders acceptance. However, when non-Christian parts of the world decide to emulate Western ideas of economic freedom they prosper. Look what happened to the economies of Taiwan, South Korea, Hong Kong, and Singapore when they turned the market economy loose!

REGARDING THE POOR

Ecclesiastical pronouncements on the economy are fond of the phrase "a preferential option for the poor." It is invoked as the rationale for governmental redistribution of wealth, that is, for a program of taxing earnings away from those who produce in order to subsidize selected groups and individuals. But it is a fact that reshuffling wealth by programs of tax and subsidy merely enriches some at the expense of others; the nation as a whole becomes poorer. Private enterprise capitalism is, in fact, the answer for anyone who really does have a preferential option for the poor. The free market economy, wherever it has been allowed to function, has elevated more poor people further out of poverty faster than any other system.

Another phrase, repeated like a mantra, is "the poor and oppressed." There is, of course, a connection between these two words; a person who is oppressed is poorer than he would be otherwise. Oppression is always political; oppression is the result of unjust laws. Correct the injustice by repealing unjust laws; establish political liberty and economic freedom. But even in the resulting free society, where people are *not* oppressed, there will still be some people who are relatively poor because of the limited demand for their services. Teachers and preachers are poor compared to rock musicians because the masses spend millions to have their ears assaulted by amplified sound, in preference to the good advice often available for free!

Ecclesiastical documents announce their concern for "the poor and oppressed," but the authors of these documents are completely blind to the forms oppression may take in our day. If there are unjust political interventions that deny people employment, this would seem to be a flagrant case of oppression. There are many such interventions. Minimum-wage laws, for instance, deny certain people access to employment, and these people are poorer than they would be otherwise; the entire nation is less well off because some people are not permitted to take a job. The same might be said of the laws that grant monopoly status to certain groups of people gathered as "unions" – U.A.W., Teamsters, and the like. The above-market wage rate they gain for union members results in unemployment for others both union and non-union. It is not difficult to figure out why this is so. The general principle is that when something begins to cost more we tend to use less of it. So, when labor begins to cost more, fewer workers will be hired.

It would take several pages to list all of the alphabet agencies that regulate, control, and hinder productivity, making the entire nation less prosperous than it need be. Our country suffers under these oppressions, economically and otherwise, but not so severely as the oppressed people of other nations, especially Communist and Third World nations. Churchmen recommend, as a cure for Third World poverty, that we deprive the already overtaxed and hampered productive segment of our people of an even larger portion of their earnings, so as to turn more of our money over to Third World governments. This will further empower the very Third World politicians who are even now oppressing their people, enabling those autocrats to oppress them more efficiently!

THE NEW TESTAMENT AND THE RICH

It is not difficult to rebut the manifestoes issued by various religious organizations. But then we turn to certain New Testament writings and are confronted by what seem to be condemnations of the rich. How, for example, shall we understand Jesus' remark, found in Luke 18:25 and Matthew 19:24: "It is easier for a camel to go through a needle's eye, than for a rich man to enter into the kingdom of God"?

Jesus' listeners were astonished when they heard these words. Worldly prosperity, many of them assumed, was a mark of God's favor. It seemed to follow that the man whom God favored with riches in this life was thereby guaranteed a spot in heaven in the next.

There is a grain of truth in this distorted popular mentality. Biblical religion holds that man is a created being, with the signature of his Creator written on each person's soul. This inner sacredness implies the ideal of liberty and justice in the relations between person and person. These free people are given dominion over the earth in order to subdue it, working "for the glory of the Creator and the relief of man's estate," as Francis Bacon put it. This is but another way of saying that those who follow the natural order of things – God's order – in ethics and economics will do better for themselves than those who violate this order. The faithful, we read in Job 36:11, ". . . if they obey and serve Him . . . shall spend their days in prosperity and their years in pleasures."

Perhaps Jesus had something else in mind as well. Palestine had been conquered by Rome. Roman overlords, wielding power and enriching themselves at the expense of the local population, would certainly supply many examples of "a rich man." Furthermore, there were those among the subject people who hired themselves out as publicans to serve the Romans by extorting taxes from their fellow Jews. "Publicans and sinners" is virtually one word in the Gospels!

In nearly every nation known to history, rulers have used their political power to seize the wealth produced by others for the gratification of themselves and their friends. Kings and courtiers in the days of slavery and serfdom consumed much of the wealth produced by farmers, artisans, and craftsmen. Today, politicians in Communist, socialist, and welfarist nations, democratically elected by "the people," share their power with a congeries of special interests, factions, and pressure groups who systematically prey on the economy, depriving people who do the world's work of over 40 percent of everything they earn.

Many a "rich man" lives on legal plunder, today as well as in times past. Frederic Bastiat's little book, *The Law*, familiarizes us with the procedure. The law is an instrument of justice, intended to secure each individual in his right to his life, his liberty, and his rightful property. Ownership is rightfully claimed as the fruit of honest toil and/or as the result of voluntary exchanges of goods and services. But the law, as Bastiat points out, is perverted from an instrument of justice into a device of plunder when it takes goods from lawful owners by legislative fiat and transfers them to groups of the politically powerful. Political plunder is a species of theft. The fact that it is legally sanctioned does not make it morally right; it is a violation of the commandment against theft.

The Israelites had fond memories of King Solomon. "All through his reign," we read in I Kings 4:25, "Judah and Israel continued at peace, every man under his own vine and fig tree, from Dan to Beersheba." A nice tribute to individual ownership and economic well-being! The Bible has high praise for honestly earned wealth, and it is exceedingly unlikely that Jesus, in the passage we have been considering, intended anything like a general condemnation of wealth, as such.

At this point someone might raise a legitimate question: "Did not Jesus say, in the Sermon on the Mount, 'Blessed are the poor'?" Well, yes and no. The Sermon on the Mount appears in two of the four Gospels, in Matthew and in Luke. In Luke 6:20 the Beatitude reads: "Blessed are the poor"; but in Matthew 5:3 it is: "Blessed are the poor *in spirit.*" There's a discrepancy here; how shall we interpret it?

The Beatitudes were spoken somewhere between 25 and 30 A.D. The Gospels of Matthew and Luke appeared some 50 or 60 years later. Both authors had access to the Gospel of Mark, to fragments of other writings now lost, and to an oral tradition extending over the generations. We do not have the original manuscripts of the Gospels; what we have are copies of copies, and eventually translations of copies into various languages.

Scholars tell us that the Aramaic original of those two words, "the poor," is *am ha-aretz* – "*people* of the land." The *am ha-aretz* – at this stage in Israel's history – were outside the tribal system of Jewish society; they did not have the time or inclination to observe the niceties of priestly law, let alone its scribal elaborations. The work of the *am ha-aretz* brought them into contact with Gentiles and Gentile ways of life, which in the eyes of the orthodox was defiling. Their status is like that of the people on the bottom rung of the Hindu caste system – the *Sudras*. Jesus is reminding His hearers that these outcasts are equal in God's sight to anyone else in Israel, and because of their lowly station in the eyes of society, they may be more open to man's need of God than the proud people in the ranks above them. The New English Bible provides an interesting slant on this text; it translates "poor in spirit" as "those who know their need of God."

In short, Jesus is saying that all are equally precious in God's sight, including the lowly *am ha-aretz*; He is not praising indigence, as such.

BIBLICAL INTERPRETATION

The Bible is full of metaphor and symbolism and allegory. Literal interpretation usually falls short; proper interpretation demands a bit of finesse . . . as in the case of St. Paul's remark about money.

St. Paul declared that "The love of money is the root of all evil" (I Tim. 6:10). The word "money" in this context – scholars tell us – does not mean coins, or bonds, or a bank account. Paul uses the word "money" to symbolize the secular world's pursuit of wealth and power. We tend to become infatuated with "the world." It's the infatuation which is evil, for God's kingdom is not wholly of this world. We are the kind of creatures whose ultimate destiny is achieved only in another order of reality: "Here we have no continuing city" (Heb. 13:14). Accept this world with all *its* joys and delights; live it to the full; but remember – we are pilgrims, not settlers. In today's vernacular, Paul might be telling us: "Have a love affair with this world, but don't marry it!"

We know that there are numerous unlawful ways to get rich, and these deserve condemnation. But prosperity also comes to a man or woman as the fairly earned reward of honest effort and service. The Bible has nothing but praise for wealth thus gained. "Seest thou a man diligent in his business?" said the author of Proverbs (Prov. 22:29). "He shall stand before kings." Economic well-being is everyone's birthright, provided it is the result of honest effort. But we are warned against a false philosophy of material possessions.

This, I think, is the point of Jesus' parable of the rich man whose crops were so good that he had to build bigger barns (Luke 12:17). This good fortune was the man's excuse for saying, "Soul, thou hast much goods laid up for many years; take thine ease, eat, drink, be merry."

There is a twofold point to this parable. The first is that nothing in life justifies us in resigning from life; we must never stop growing. It has been well said that we don't grow old, we *become* old by not growing. The second point is that a material windfall – like falling heir to a million dollars – may tempt a man into the error of quitting the struggle for the real goals in life. Jesus condemned the man who put his trust in riches, who "layeth up treasure for himself and is not rich toward God." He did not condemn material possessions as such; He taught stewardship, which is the responsible ownership and use of rightfully acquired material goods.

Life here is probative; our three score years and ten are a sort of test run. As St. Augustine put it, "We are here schooled for life eternal." And one of the important examination questions concerns our economic use of the planet's scarce resources and the proper management of our material possessions. These are the twin facets of Christian stewardship, and poor performance here will result in dire consequences. Jesus put it very strongly: "If, therefore, you have not been faithful in the use of worldly wealth, who will entrust to you the true riches?" (Luke 16:12)

What does it mean to be "faithful in the use of worldly wealth?" What else can it mean except the intelligent and responsible use of the planet's scarce resources to transform them by human effort and ingenuity into the consumable goods we humans require not only for survival, but also as a means for the finer things in life? In practice, this means free market capitalism – the free enterprise system – in the production, exchange, and utilization of our material wealth in the service of our chosen goals.

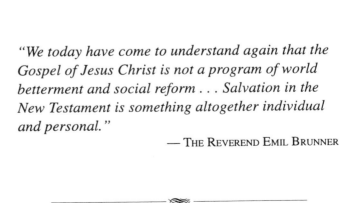

"We today have come to understand again that the Gospel of Jesus Christ is not a program of world betterment and social reform . . . Salvation in the New Testament is something altogether individual and personal."

— THE REVEREND EMIL BRUNNER

CHAPTER THREE

ETHICS AND THE WELFARE STATE

An official highly placed in the former Socialist government of Great Britain reportedly attributed a significant measure of his party's success to the teachings of England's churches. There has been, both in England and in America, a highly articulate body of churchmen for whom a Christian social order means nothing less than Socialism. Many of these theologians have hailed the religious significance of Karl Marx; one of them has said of Marxism that it "will provide the only possible property system compatible with the necessities of a technical age."

Other churchmen who have been repelled by the materialism of Marx embraced a program which was promised as a middle course between the extremes of Capitalism and Socialism. This middle ground was, by many, likened unto the social experiments in American life which bore the labels of New Deal and Fair Deal.

YARDSTICK OF THE GOSPELS

The point of reference for these men, as for all Christians, is contained in the teachings of Jesus. If Jesus' ethics cannot become normative for men except in a Socialist commonwealth, then all men who desire Jesus' ethics to prevail are under obligation to work toward a collectivist society. Such is the driving force behind those churchmen who have embraced the Social Gospel. But on the other hand, if a Socialist society in actual operation would necessarily and continuously nullify the ethics of Jesus, the believers in that ethic are constrained to work toward the establishment of a free society whose institutions would strive to conform to the mandates of the gospels.

Jesus laid down two great and inseparable commandments. The first is to "love the Lord thy God with all thy heart, and with all thy soul, and with all thy mind." There are powerful forces in the soul which conflict with this commandment. Foremost is the tendency in each man to construct a system of meanings with himself at the center. The idea that there is outside him something fixed, which he can neither buy, bribe, tamper with nor control, is an affront to human pride. That the individual can find his true life only in conformity with the movement and purpose of this something outside, is a further deflation of his pride. But a necessary preliminary to the proper orientation of personal life is to be driven to these conclusions. Men are dependent creatures, according to Jesus, whose principle of existence lies not in themselves but in God. They are the stewards of a gift of life, and will be judged on their stewardship – not by men but by God. And frequently, He said, "that which is highly esteemed among men is abomination in the sight of God."

What men will do with that which they have been lent is a matter of personal decision, the consequences of which no man can escape. The servant in the parable who wrapped his talent in a napkin and hid it in the ground, was deprived of that talent and it was given to him whose record of stewardship was best. Reality will not accommodate itself to us. It has its own terms and they are self-enforcing. "Narrow is the way which leadeth unto life, and few there be that find it."

The second commandment, said Jesus, is like unto the first: "Thou shalt love thy neighbor as thyself." We are enjoined first of all to love God with our whole being; any interpretation of the second commandment must take this into account. Furthermore, the second commandment is not simply an injunction to love your neighbor, but to love your neighbor as yourself. There is nothing in this commandment to suggest that we ought to be our brother's keeper; nor is the brother's keeper idea contained in any part of Biblical teaching. Finally, this second commandment should not be confused with that disguised egoism for which Auguste Comte more than a century ago coined the word "altruism."

TRUE NEIGHBORLINESS

The order in which the two great commandments are given suggest that true neighborliness and genuine community follow the individual's discovery of his real self in relation to God. Augustine bears out this thought when he speaks of the "harmonious enjoyment of God and of one another in God." Without an understanding of the aim and purpose of personal life given in the first commandment, the man to man relationship becomes a self-conscious effort to sacrifice what is thought to be a personal good for the intended benefit of another man. The determination to "do good" to our fellow man frequently betrays us into smugness on the one side and resentment on the other; the intended benefit rarely materializes.

True neighborliness recognizes an obligation to one's fellow man, because he, like one's self, is included in the purposes of the Eternal, and hence is a creature of infinite worth and dignity. This is all the warrant one needs for refusing to impose his will on another, and for resisting the imposition of an alien will over his own.

How do these two great commandments square with the mechanics of a Socialist order? Proponents of collectivist measures, when these are urged on the basis of their Christian motivation, speak of them in terms of human welfare. Welfare state legislation is said to carry out our obligation to our neighbor, using the instrumentality of government as an efficient means of doing our Christian duty. But consider the mechanics of what happens in the so-called welfare state.

Those who believe that government is simply an effective bit of machinery through which charitable impulses can be made to go further and do more good form a tiny minority. The welfare projects which they would like to have government undertake are extensive, so extensive that they cannot be carried out unless this tiny minority can secure the participation of the vast majority. So the minority, composed of Socialists or welfarestaters, secures the passage of laws which force reluctant citizens to participate in socialistic schemes against their wills or suffer penalties for refusing. The Socialist is prepared to use legal violence where necessary to penalize people whose only crime is that they haven't been persuaded that Socialistic means are the right ones to use to obtain social advance and individual betterment. Legal penalties which are legitimate when used against criminals to protect peaceful citizens, are questionable, to say the least, when used against peaceful citizens. Yet these are the means which Socialists and collectivists must employ.

SOME ONE GETS HURT

Consider the case of a housing project. Better housing for all people is certainly a desirable goal to work for. The welfarestater decides that government should undertake the building of houses. But houses cannot be built without money, even by government, so the welfarestater must invoke the coercive powers of government to get it. The money is obtained under duress by taxation which deprives people of their property for purposes most of them cannot endorse. This group is "afflicted . . . in mind, body, or estate" to the extent that its members have their wills imposed upon and their property taken from them. They are forced to do what they cannot be persuaded to do, and this is an invasion of their liberty. Furthermore, they are deprived of property which is rightfully theirs, not for a community purpose or for the common good, but for the express benefit of a selected minority. Thus the Socialist or the welfare stater when he puts his schemes into operation, inevitably hurts some people in his efforts to help other people.

Socialism supposedly stems from the emotion of altruism, which is thought be more more commendable than egotism. But in point of fact, altruism is a deadlier egotism. It heightens self-consciousness in a creature with a capacity and an urge for self-transcendence. True neighborliness, as Jesus conceived it, was an overflow from the fullness of life consequent upon the personal quest for God. True self-fulfillment results in men whose efforts produce a by-product which benefits their fellows without injuring them. John Bunyan, for example, made no pretense of writing his "Pilgrim's Progress" for the benefit of his fellows. In the Apology for the work he wrote, ". . . nor did I undertake thereby to please my neighbor; no, not I. I did it mine own self to gratify." But he created a masterpiece which still enriches human life.

In this connection it is interesting to note that in Jesus' parable of the last judgment, those who are called righteous are utterly unconscious of their righteousness. "When saw we thee and hungered and fed thee?" they say. There is apparently nothing self-conscious in the highest morality. Altruism is a self-conscious righteousness, which, like self-conscious art, bears the stigmata of degeneracy. It is this self-conscious righteousness which the welfarestater seeks to put behind his political planning when he advocates socialistic measures on religious grounds. This is a use of religion as fuel to stoke the fires of social change, and it shifts the emphasis of religion from personal transformation to social reform. On the one hand, this tends to make religion merely conventional, a prop to the social order. And on the other hand, the social order becomes one in which some men are deliberately put at the disposal of other men.

Merely conventional religion, Jesus pointed out, like merely conventional righteousness, might also be a blind alley for the human spirit when it is used by a group to sanction the idea that they have captured God for their side. It was this use of religion by the Pharisees which evoked from Jesus some of his bitterest denunciations. Devotion to the externals of religion is not acceptable as a substitute for the cultivation of its true inwardness.

Once the claims of the higher life really lay their demands upon the individual, all else becomes secondary. Once the hand is set to the plow there is no turning back; let the dead bury the dead, turn from father and mother, where there was peace introduce a sword – if there be interference with the mandates of the burgeoning life within.

Righteousness, religion, and also riches may obstruct and stifle man's true life. The danger in religion and righteousness is the complacency they induce; it is a little religion and a little righteousness that divert us from pursuit of the real thing. The danger in the possession of wealth is that it may be taken as a false indication of the health of the soul. This is the point of Jesus' parable of the rich man whose crops were so good that he had to build bigger barns. This good fortune the man took to be a warrant for saying, "Soul, thou hast much goods laid up for many years! Take thine ease, eat, drink, be merry." The twofold point in the parable is that nothing in life justifies a man in assuming this attitude, and that a material windfall may tempt men to fall into the error of concluding their striving for the real goal of life. Jesus condemned the man who "layeth up treasure for himself and is not rich toward God," which is not the same as condemning material possessions or wealth held under proper stewardship. He said, "If, therefore, you have not been faithful in the use of worldly wealth, who will entrust to you the true riches?"

A NEW KIND OF LIFE

Jesus did not come to introduce a new set of rules, but to live a new kind of life and set forth the claims and demands of that new life as only a living example of it could do. And he indicted all those things which minister to human pride and induce accommodation and adjustment to the second and third rate.

The concept of a government so limited as to allow individuals scope to fulfill their religious obligations to God and their fellow men is compatible with the Christian belief in the worth and dignity of persons. But Christian Socialism is a contradiction in terms, and the mechanics of the welfare state involve a continuous violation of personality.

The case for Christian Socialism has sometimes been urged on the grounds that Jesus condemned wealth. It is true that Jesus had a great deal to say about the conflict between serving God and serving mammon, and about the deceitfulness of riches. But it is important, if we would make an effort to assess accurately the mind of Jesus and the moralists on the subject of wealth, that certain basic considerations be first understood.

First of all, property is a relation that men have to certain bits of matter. In some religions matter as such is evil, delusive, opposed to the good principle of mind or spirit. This dualism is obvious in some Oriental religions, and it has appeared as a heresy in Christendom from time to time in odd cults. The idea that matter is evil puts material possessions at a discount, and a society of Manicheans, for instance, would have little interest in framing a code for the protection of private property, nor would it put the seal of virtue on thrift. But for Christianity the material world is good, as the doctrines of Creation and the Incarnation testify. In Christian thought, it is not the spirit which is corrupted by matter, but the reverse; corruption stems from the spiritual, from the stubborn God-deflecting will of man.

In the second place, thoughtful persons are painfully aware of the ugly human traits of avarice and miserliness. When the normal human desire for a competence becomes inflamed, and energy is bent solely toward the accumulation of more and more material possessions, we are in the presence of a perversion which needs therapy. What is perverted is the proper stewardship of human energy.

The Moralist and Political Privilege

The third and most important consideration for one who would bring the concepts of property and wealth within the purview of moral principles, is a larger understanding of political and economic theory than most moralists have ever displayed. In most countries of the world throughout recorded history, the bureaucrats of the political agency have intervened in the nation's economy to grant some men a political privilege at the expense of other men. This has everywhere enabled a few men to become rich by the degradation of other men who were thereby forced to live in poverty. The ire of the prophet and moralist has rightfully been roused by this circumstance, but his emotion did not mean that the moralist diagnosed the situation accurately. For the most part, he condemned riches or rich men when he should have condemned the political means which enabled some men to accumulate wealth as parasites upon other men. As long as the State, the agency of coercion, stands over society offering to dispense economic privilege to those who pay it homage, conferring an advantage on some men at the expense of other men the misuse of political power should be the first line of attack for the moralist. It is inevitable that political privilege will be used in this way if it is available and begging to be used. No people has ever resisted it who have been led into this temptation. And whether the exercise of political privilege puts five dollars into a man's pocket, or five million, it is the political transaction which is the major evil, not the fact that some men profit by it to a larger extent than others.

These considerations apply to any effort to understand what Jesus meant by what he said about wealth. Palestine was an occupied country, a Roman province, and people who obtain wealth under those circumstances do so by playing ball with the conquerors. It is not difficult, when the political power is wielded by foreigners, for the subject people to be aware of the tainted source of the wealth of certain of their fellow citizens. Palestinians knew that this wealth was not accumulated by industry and thrift, but largely by accepting Roman favors.

Jesus did not teach that material things are evil in themselves; he did not urge the relinquishment of all property relationships. Only in one case, that of the rich young ruler, did he urge a man to divest himself of all his wealth. In this particular case we may assume that Jesus perceived that the rich young ruler had a perverted attachment to wealth. For him it was a poison, just as for the members of Alcoholic Anonymous, alcohol is a poison and not just a narcotic. If something is a poison for a man, the only sane thing to do is to abjure it altogether, not to try to take it in small doses. It is entirely possible that some men cannot put themselves to the job of making money without having their souls blighted in the process. Perhaps there should be for such people an organization called Misers Anonymous. A miser is one who puts his trust in riches, not simply one who is rich. Jesus said, "How hard it is for them that trust in riches to enter into the kingdom of God." (Mk. 10:25), which is not to discuss those who have riches.

Jesus emphasized, as moralists of all ages have done, the temptations that surround material possessions. But where there is no temptation and testing there is no virtue. There is a proper accommodation of the human spirit toward material things; they are items to be mastered, and we master them by practicing a philosophy of non-attachment or "holy indifference" toward them. The more efficiently we can produce to satisfy our creature needs the more energy is released to enable us to attend to the things we are really here for, the things of the spirit. If we have been seduced by the philosophy that the accumulation of material things is what matters most, we will not find a cure for it by making it harder for men to meet their creaturely needs by putting political burdens upon industry. Wealth is only a matter of degree, and it is just as easy to be infected with a false philosophy of material possession over a thousand dollars as over a million.

OUR NEIGHBOR'S NEED

Rich and poor are relative terms, but Jesus recognized that there would always be some people who will need the help of those able to administer it. He stressed the importance of almsgiving, and said: "It is more blessed to give than to receive." (Acts 20:35) If Jesus regarded as important the blessing that comes to one who voluntarily renders help, then the churches have been right in presenting the claims of philanthropy as one of the most important of religious obligations. For one thing, this obligation keeps us sensitive and aware toward an important aspect of our environment – other peoples' needs. Secondly, this is a rightful stewardship of one's own property, and it is the antithesis of the practice whereby one man volunteers another man's property for use in alleviating some real or imagined distress – as in various schemes of social security.

This point needs to be stressed because of the current contrary emphasis. The prevailing view in certain circles is expressed by a theologian who is a member of the executive council of Christian Action. He writes that the Christian will rejoice "that by the mechanism of government he can feed the hungry, clothe the naked, and love his brethren in practical ways." (Alexander Miller, *The Christian Significance of Karl Marx*, Pp. 90-91) That the coercive redistribution of property should be called an equivalent of "the law of Christ" to "bear one another's burdens" (Gal. 6:2) is an example of what happens when theology is tailored to fit partisan purposes. "We then that are strong," said Paul, "ought to bear the infirmities of the weak." (Rom. 15:1) But Paul was aware that a weakness in the will might overcome strength in the back, so that some people would mistake their own laziness for weakness and allow themselves to be carried along by others. So he added, "Everyone will have to carry his own load." (Gal. 6:5) "The man who stole must not steal any more; he must work with his hands at honest toil instead, so as to have something to share with those who are in need." (Eph. 4:28) There is nothing in any of these admonitions to help our neighbor which can possibly be construed as sanctioning the use of political coercion to deprive some men of what is rightfully theirs for the dubious benefit of someone else.

SANCTITY OF THE PERSON

But it is not so much in selected verses that the fundamental opposition between Biblical ethics and the welfare state idea is revealed. It is in the fact of the incompatibility of the basic Christian ethics with the philosophy and practices of the welfare state. The late Archbishop Temple has said that "The primary principle of Christian Ethics and Christian Politics must be respect for every person simply as a person." These words of the Archbishop would find wide acceptance, and their import is in conflict with the planning of a welfare state, or socialism, which cannot be effected except by giving some men political power over the lives and energies of other men. In a socialistic commonwealth by its very nature some men must be the creatures of other men. There is no word magic by which this situation can be squared with the basic teachings of the Bible.

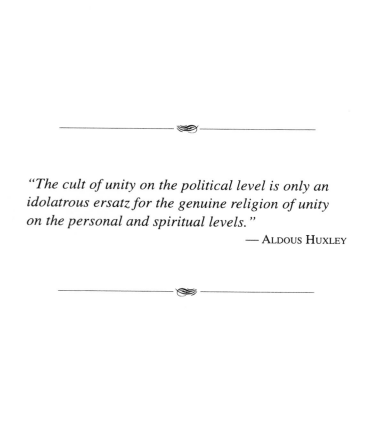

"The cult of unity on the political level is only an idolatrous ersatz for the genuine religion of unity on the personal and spiritual levels."

— ALDOUS HUXLEY

CHAPTER FOUR

THE ECUMENICAL MOVEMENT AND SOCIAL ACTION

Christian unity is both a present fact and a future ideal. There is genuine Christian unity linking individuals and churches all over the world in one great family of churches. On a deeper level, and even more broadly based, there is a unity of the peoples who affirm a religious view of life as distinguished from those who reject a religious view. The substratum of the world religions is the faith that there is a spiritual ground to all reality, and that there is a moral order which is part of the very structure of the universe. Christianity embraces, but far transcends, this substratum. It would be difficult indeed to gain universal assent to a set of propositions which constitute the basic affirmations of Christianity, but the following five propositions, which represent the least common denominator of the beliefs of Christians of all communions, would probably find wide acceptance. These basic Christian principles are: 1) God as Creator and Father; 2) Jesus Christ as the unique revelation of God in history; 3) The Church as a human institution divinely commissioned; 4) The unique value of the Bible; 5) The importance of Christianity to personal and social morality.

These are the cords which hold all Christians together. This is the reality of Christian unity. This is the soil in which the ecumenical movement has taken root, and without which that movement would not be. This is the important part of the present fact.

The lesser part of the present fact concerns the surface and subsurface movements in world Christianity which have resulted in the world conference at Amsterdam where the World Council of Churches was formed, and the Second Assembly of the World Council of Churches held in Evanston, Illinois, in August, 1954.

BASIC CHRISTIAN UNITY

The existence of a foundational unity among Christians everywhere, gave rise, nearly half a century ago, to the articulate demand for the creation of an agency which could function for the churches in matters in which there is substantial agreement. Tentative exploratory gestures toward the creation of such an agency were begun in 1910 at an international missionary conference held in Edinburgh. Several international conferences later, in 1948, the World Council of Churches was born. This is an agency constituted by 161 churches or denominations which fall into 19 broad ecclesiastical groupings. The World Council does not pretend to be a super-church and has no formal authority over the church bodies associated with it. Its influence, however, is considerable.

The World Council is a continuing organization with offices in New York, London and Geneva. It has six presidents and ninety members of its central committee from all over the globe. This body of ninety-six meets annually in various parts of the world. An executive committee of twelve members meets semiannually. Scheduled to meet every five years is the World Council of Churches Assembly, composed of 600 delegates from the member churches, plus 150 consultants, 100 youth delegates, and accredited visitors. This is the Assembly which met in Evanston. In the United States the American wing of the World Council is an organization of 29 member churches headed by Bishop G. Bromley Oxnam. [1956]

The first Assembly meeting at Amsterdam selected as its theme "Man's Disorder and God's Design," and divided this theme into four great topics: 1) The Universal Church in God's Design; 2) The

Church's Witness to God's Design; 3) The Church and the Disorder of Society; 4) The Church and the International Disorder.

The theme of the Evanston Assembly was "Christ – The Hope of the World." The subsidiary themes were six in number: 1) Faith and Order; 2) Evangelism; 3) Social Questions; 4) International Affairs; 5) Intergroup Relations; 6) The Laity.

Merely to read the topics listed above is to realize that the ecumenical movement carries with it some subject matter whose immediate relevance to the quest for a united Christendom is not at first glance apparent, nor at second glance either. A study of the Amsterdam and Evanston reports confirms the impression that the ecumenical movement carries some impedimenta.

DUBIOUS BAGGAGE

An ecumenical movement must take account of the fact of such Christian unity as exists; it must create channels for the more effective expression of that unity; it must seek to provide scope and tolerance for individual differences; it must seek to place our differences in perspective so that the little things which separate us shall not be held so close to our eyes as to blot out from our vision the big things that bind us together. All of these necessary and valuable functions the ecumenical movement provides to some degree. But no organization deserves praise for doing no more than sitting on its laurels. The matters concerning which there is unity should be a platform for launching ideas not yet generally held. There should be an area for experiment and debate and testing. If there is dubious baggage in a movement, it is justified only if it is there for proper weighing and assaying. In other words, if ecumenicity is to be a movement, and not simply a monument, it needs a growing edge at which there are things that are tentative, and even doubtful. But if a movement needs doubtful features in order that it may grow, there must be liberty so that the doubtful features can prove themselves one way or the other.

There is a fine old slogan which ought to be emblazoned on the masthead of every discussion which involves deep personal feelings, such as a discussion of the ecumenical movement. It reads, "In necessary things unity, in doubtful things liberty, in everything charity." There is, up to a significant level, a genuine Christian unity. It is a unity in necessary things and it is real. Without it, not even the idea of ecumenicity would have dawned. Because of it, the ecumenical movement came into being and resulted in the creation of the World Council of Churches.

The question that needs to be raised now is whether or not the doubtful baggage that fastened itself onto the agenda of the international gatherings which gave birth to the World Council furthers, or even serves, the cause of Christian unity. By "doubtful baggage" reference is made especially to the subsidiary themes numbered three and four above: Social Questions and International Affairs.

The churchmen, lay and clerical, who participated in the international church conferences from 1910 on, were children of the age, and so are we all. Thus it was inevitable that they should bring to the thinking, discussing and resolving of each conference certain secular assumptions and dogmas which have no causal relation to their religion. Churchmen, and others as well, have always tended to adopt the protective coloration of their era. Thus, to a fifteenth century conference they would have brought dogmas about the flatness of the earth, which have no necessary relation to the Faith. A century later, dogmas about the divine right of kings would have the same unquestioning acceptance, and an effort would be made to give these dogmas a logical place in the great Christian scheme. In the seventeenth century they innocently and unquestioningly accepted the fact of witches. And in the twentieth century they brought to the conferences two of the most beguiling assumptions of our time.

The first of these is that there should be one world of manmade law whose precepts are to be enforced on reluctant people, if that prove necessary, by an international political body. The second assumption is that government should be freed from the shackles placed upon it in the philosophy and practice of historic Liberalism so that it might play a more active role in regulating economic life and thus bring about a social levelling. Both these assumptions stem from a common root, the axiom that political action, i.e. legalized violence, has an efficacy in human affairs far surpassing uncoerced, voluntary action.

THE GREAT SECULAR FAITH

The creation of a powerful, extensive and centralized government with a ubiquitous bureaucracy is an essential ingredient of nearly all the viable schemes of social uplift of our time. The belief that when this political agency is powerful enough to act despite the obstructionist tactics of the reactionaries it will bring about the kingdom of heaven on earth, is the great secular faith of the modern world. This is the faith of many churchmen as well, although it has no necessary connection with Christian doctrines. And because this faith cannot be put into operation without doing deliberate injury to selected innocent groups of people, it would seem to involve a necessary conflict with Christian ethics. These are the "doubtful things" which have attached themselves to the movement: to find more effective ways of giving expression to Christian unity.

For reasons of space, and because I believe the domestic issues are more fundamental (political interventions create economic and other dislocations in a nation which ripen the conditions under which that nation will consent to be dragged into a career of international meddling), this paper will deal only with the internal political interventions which might be called socialism or collectivism had they a full blown philosophy. Of the philosophy falsely called "Internationalism" only this needs to be said. Before the era of so-called "Internationalism," that is, before the first World War, almost every part of the world was open to almost every person. Anyone with the urge and the means to travel could go wherever he chose, and he did not need a passport. It was a world without refugees.* Now, half a century, 25 million dead, 49 million wounded, 44 million missing and 1500 billion dollars later, the freedom to move about is severely restricted, goods move across frontiers only after hurdling high tariff barriers, there are millions of refugees and the world is virtually without a place of refuge. In spite of the terrible evidence that those who call themselves Internationalists or One-Worlders are on the wrong track, serious discussion of the issues is *verboten* everywhere, suppressed by the Internationalists themselves. The Internationalist creed has affixed itself to the ecumenical movement.

Collectivism has a long history and there have been articulate collectivists among the clergy for at least as far back as the Christian Socialist movement in England more than a century ago. Maurice and Kingsley were the leaders of this trend which has been influential down to the present day. It was from Kingsley that Marx borrowed the phrase about religion being the opiate of the people. In America, the native Social Gospel movement dates from the gilded age of the post-Civil War period. Both movements attracted able and high-minded men who perceived correctly that our western society had some cancerous spots in it. One is forced to be critical of their diagnosis and remedy – not enough government, therefore social legislation – but all the same they were several cuts above their contemporaries who preached a gospel of material progress and fatuously bleated that nothing was wrong. The social gospellers wanted to strengthen the hand of the state so that it could cope with various social injustices, whereas if their diagnosis had gone deep enough they would have detected a misuse of political power at the base of the very injus-

---

*The 1990's version of "Free Trade" relates to taxes, not freedom of exchange between buyer and seller, which – today – is more regulated than ever before. (Ed.)

tices of which they complained. In these cases, either government was doing what government should not do – aiding some at
the expense of others, or it was not doing what government should
do – enforcing the laws against predation.

THE SOCIAL GOSPEL AND CHURCH UNITY

As scattered voices, the social gospellers were ineffective. They
perceived that if they were going to have any effect on politicians
they must present a united front; they must work for church unity
so that the churches could act as a sounding board when the
social gospellers spoke to legislators. C. H. Hopkins points out in
his book *The Rise of the Social Gospel* that "The influence of the
social gospel upon movements toward the unity of the churches
was an important aspect of the rise of social Christianity . . . the
federative movements that came into being around the turn of
the century were based on social-active impulses rather than creedal
or doctrinal agreement." Robert Bilheimer in his book *The Quest
for Christian Unity* says that the movements for unity stemmed
from "a concern which in fact did not stir the mass of church
membership greatly, but chiefly the leadership of the churches.
Local councils and the Federal Council of Churches of Christ in
America alike had their origin mainly in the response of church
leadership to the evils of industrial society. The first of the city
councils of churches were organized principally to combat in a
united way the problems created by industrialism . . . (the) main
impetus came from those who were principally concerned with
the moral life of the nation and the impact of the churches on
the social order . . . From its establishment in 1908 until its
merger in 1950 into the National Council of Churches, The Federal Council of Churches of Christ in America . . . maintained a
strong insistence upon the need for bringing the Christian conscience to bear upon the problems of social injustice. It was a
rallying point for all concerned with the social gospel."

Two other authorities may be cited to further reveal the mind-set of the men who were the moving spirits in the establishment of the old Federal Council and the world-wide trend toward church union. Henry F. May writes in *Protestant Churches and Industrial America*, "In this federation (the Federal Council) representing the liberal elements in all denominations, Social Gospel advocates were able to put American Protestantism officially and repeatedly on record in comparatively concrete terms as a warm supporter of labor's cause." And Liston Pope, writing in *Christian Faith and Social Action* says, "The social expectations of the Social Gospel leaders were not untypical of the age . . . The organization of the Methodist Federation for Social Service in 1907 and the Federal Council of Churches in 1908 reflected these purposes and gave institutional form to efforts for their realization."

The social actionists in the churches worked with comparatively little publicity until 1948. Then came Amsterdam. The most famous sentence to come out of the Amsterdam Assembly of 1948 reads as follows: "The Christian churches should reject the ideologies of both communism and laissez-faire capitalism, and should seek to draw men away from the false assumption that these extremes are the only alternatives." Whatever else this sentence demonstrates, it reveals that the social-actionist wing of churchmen had been at work in the ecumenical movement. And they are at work still. The Evanston study pamphlet on this subject says, "We are not lacking in theory, in the articulation of fundamental principles. These are the fruits of four decades of ecumenical endeavor which we inherit: Stockholm and Oxford; Lausanne and Edinburgh (1937); Edinburgh (1910); Jerusalem, Madras and Whitby."

THE RESPONSIBLE SOCIETY

The concept of a Responsible Society, the Amsterdam phrase for a middle ground for Christians between Communism and Capitalism something like the British Labor government, is the fruition of a century of action by many churchmen trying to come up with an answer for social grievances.

There is nothing sinister in the activities of these men; they are men with a strong set of beliefs who seek to implement them as best they know. Leadership has been assumed by men of position and character commanding enormous resources in the Christian Church; not by Communists or subversives. The philosophy of a Responsible Society stands or falls on its own merits; it will not topple merely because some fragment smells a little like Marx.

This paper has sought to establish two points. First, that there is a genuine Christian unity which preceded the ecumenical movement and upon which the ecumenical movement built as a foundation. Second, that ecumenicity, the drive for church unity has been sparked largely by men whose social actionist philosophy is collectivist, i.e., requires extensive political intervention into the everyday affairs of men. There are other aspects of the ecumenical movement, but our inquiry is limited to the question of whether or not the "doubtful thing" of a collectivist social philosophy adds strength to the cause of church unity or is an impediment to unity.

One cannot wholly blame the ecclesiastical collectivists that during the past century the concepts of the social gospel were not hammered out in conjunction with libertarians who would have a differing set of convictions about what constitutes the Responsible Society. There were very few libertarians around. Now there are many, and they have competently pointed out the many un-Christian and immoral features of every variety of collectivism, including Christian Socialism. This challenge by the libertarians has been largely ignored by churchmen in the ecumenical movement. Even today it is only rarely that a social actionist churchman condescends to talk things over on equal terms with one who professes libertarian views. Furthermore, it is not evident that any of the social actionist churchmen have spent as much time on economics as a more complete understanding of even their own position would warrant. This is true of even so influential a writer in church circles as R. H. Tawney, author of *Religion and the Rise of Capitalism*. Tawney repeats the hoariest and most often exploded economic fallacies with the air of a discoverer and with his usual charm. Apparently this has been called to his attention a number of times because in his new book *Attack and Other Papers*, he airily dismisses the matter by saying that he never had time to study the economists as they deserve. What is true in the case of Tawney is doubly true of every other writer in the social actionist camp; they are not prejudiced by acquaintance with the facts of economics.

NO CHRISTIAN ACCENT

It is also a matter for comment that the social actionist movement among churchmen for the past century or so has walked hand in hand with the secular intelligentsia when it came to theories of social reconstruction. There is no distinctive Christian accent in the Amsterdam report on a Responsible Society. It is a straight welfare state platform garnished with references to the Deity. It does not even take into account the outspokenly Christian and provocative social thought that has come from Thibon and Mounier in France, and in England from such men as Belloc and Chesterton, Gill and Penty. We are forced to conclude that in this doubtful matter of a social philosophy for the ecumenical movement there has not been full liberty of discussion nor a desire to provide a hearing for all sides. Instead, a narrow exclusionism has been practiced.

In an even more significant manner the social actionist creed dismisses liberty. This creed urges government intervention as the means by which certain social goals are to be accomplished; it puts its blessing on state supported enterprises. But whenever

political means are used to attain social ends, every person who
believes in other means to attain the same purposes is penalized.
There is not the same freedom for his ideas as for the ideas of
those who invoke political action. In any society there is room
for many voluntary ways of doing things, but there is room for
only one political way of accomplishing the same things.

When there is an establishment of religion, that is, a state
church, supported from the tax fund, every member of a noncon-
forming church is penalized for his religious beliefs. Most American churchmen would oppose this. By freedom in religion, which
most of them endorse, they mean that it is wrong to put a man
under civil disabilities by reason of his religious faith. The civil
disabilities need not go so far as burning at the stake to arouse the
believer in freedom; any civil penalty placed upon the practice of
religious beliefs is held to be a violation of religious freedom. And
this includes being taxed to support an established church when
the taxpayer finds his spiritual guidance elsewhere. Religious freedom means that a man attends the church of his choice and
supports it according to his conscience. He does this as a matter
of right, not as a luxury to be supported on his loose change after
a religious establishment has raided his pocket by means of the
tax collector.

WHEN GOVERNMENT DOES IT

Whenever any enterprise is "established" by the state, whether it
be religion, medicine, housing, education, electrification or money
lending, the same principle holds – all believers in alternate ways
of accomplishing certain ends in religion, medicine, housing, and
so on, are penalized. They are not allowed the same freedom for
their ideas which the successful advocates of political intervention obtain for theirs. The principle of freedom which is violated
by an established church is violated when the state establishes
any enterprise. But the social actionists advocate numerous po-

litical interventions in economic life, and in so doing demand a "freedom" for their social remedies which, if the demand succeeds, would not be allowed to the ideas of those who differ with them. A genuinely free society is one where the peaceful actions of men and minorities are not penalized by suffering civil disabilities for religious, social and political convictions. A social philosophy which is not broad enough in conception to work toward guarantees of personal liberty no matter what personal belief, is not generous enough to bear the label "Christian." Advocacy of political intervention narrows the area of freedom, and when such advocacy comes from churchmen it is in contradiction to the principles on which they oppose an established church.

It is worth notice that the Amsterdam meeting should speak of "laissez-faire capitalism," and indeed that the literature of the ecumenical movement on these topics reiterates the phrase. Laissez-faire has been a descriptive term for nearly a century; it has been a smear term. Herbert Spencer, writing in the 1870's remarked that anyone who questioned the divine authority of the state has the epithets "reactionary" and "laissez-faire" thrown at him! Tactics have not changed.

According to students of the phrase, laissez-faire goes back to the jousting field. When two knights prepared to tilt against one another the signal for them to begin was the call "laissez-faire." It was the equivalent to "A fair field and no favor," or "Obey the rules and may the best man win."

In the latter part of the seventeenth century business was carried on largely under royal monopoly. The story has it that the French minister Colbert in 1680 called in some merchants and asked what the government could do to help them. One of them answered "Laissez-faire." Or, in other words, "Your job is to maintain peace and order. Do that, but remove the restrictions that are throttling us.

The social actionists use the term laissez-faire to describe the idea that man can do as he pleases and get away with it. Laissez-faire has never meant this; the word the social actionists want is *hubris*, the concept which weighed so heavily on the conscience of the Greeks and provided themes for the dramas of Aeschylus.

Gerald Heard makes a wise comment in this connection. He writes, "If you own that you do not know enough about men to be able to coerce them to become better you will have to return to laissez-faire and the consent of the governed . . . Consent of the governed means bearing with much inefficiency to avoid tyranny."

IRRESPONSIBLE STATEMENTS

A preliminary study booklet entitled *The Responsible Society* was issued for the Evanston meeting. The tone in which it is written gives some insight into the mind of those who embrace the philosophy of The Responsible Society. The author says, "The anarchy of an individualistic Capitalism can no longer be tolerated." Whatever this sentence actually means, apparently it is intended to describe the position of all who question the idea of The Responsible Society – implying that their position leans toward anarchy. And if one rejects the tenets of a Responsible Society, he is put in the awkward position of seeming to endorse a chaotic and irresponsible society.

In the same booklet, The Responsible Society is described as "a mixture of institutions and methods different from both doctrinaire Socialism and doctrinaire Capitalism." No one likes to think of himself as a doctrinaire, yet he must appear to be doctrinaire if he tries to apply principles and logic to social questions instead of being content with a comfortable middle way which merely seeks to avoid extremes.

There are yet other unpleasant characteristics ascribed to those who don't endorse the idea of The Responsible Society. They favor, not simply profits, but "uncontrolled profit seeking." All they can offer to stem the tide of Communism is a "reactionary type of economic opposition." Even of their own system of free enterprise, they are "uncritical defenders." This is not a discussion of the issues, so much as it is an impugning of those who are disposed to discuss issues.

A companion study pamphlet is written in similar vein. A few quotations will give the flavor. "The strategy of the churches in relation to Communism must be based upon the resolve to support those goals of the social revolution which are consistent with the Christian understanding of God's purpose for man . . . The social revolution which on most continents is the occasion of perplexing problems and conflicts is to be recognized in one important aspect as the rising of multitudes of exploited and neglected people against the pride and greed of the white race, against institutions of property which in both feudal and capitalistic forms have kept them in poverty and dependence." The author of the pamphlet finds that a "consistent collectivism, whether it be inspired by Communism or Fascism, and an unqualified individualism, are both incompatible with Christian goals for the person and the community." I am familiar with a number of systems of partially consistent collectivisms; but no one, to my knowledge has ever advocated an "unqualified" individualism.

This, then, is the position on social questions which reflects the thinking of ecumenical leaders. At best, the philosophy is intellectually dubious; if there were real liberty to discuss it there would be extensive amendment of the position or abandonment of it. It cannot stand up under serious inquiry. And in any case, what does the divisive effort to push a narrowly conceived collectivism have to do with the broad movement designed to seek more effective means for the expression of Christian unity?

DEIFICATION OF CAESAR

Collectivism, in its many varieties, is the great secular faith of our time. It is a faith in the efficacy of political action to accomplish social ends far beyond the capacity of uncoerced men and women in voluntary action. At one end of the scale it is a deification of Caesar; at the other it is a cynical, crafty means used by some to subject others to their will. In the modern world men have been found willing to suffer and die for this false faith. But for each willing martyr, hundreds have perished as unwilling victims of the political manias of our time, raw material for the political experiments of other people.

Many men are collectivists without being aware of it because collectivism seems to be taken into one's pores from the ideological fog of our times. Most men argue only about the degree of collectivism they are willing to embrace, few are willing to eject every trace of it from their own thinking. Opposition to collectivism starts only when it dawns upon an individual that he has enough trouble running his own life and being a steward of his own energy, and that he has no mandate from society or from God to run another's life against that person's will. Men are creatures of God, not creatures of other men. It is not easy to see how inclusion of the opposite philosophy in the ecumenical movement can add strength to the ties that bind men in Christian love.

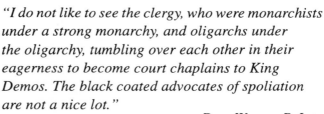

*"I do not like to see the clergy, who were monarchists
under a strong monarchy, and oligarchs under
the oligarchy, tumbling over each other in their
eagerness to become court chaplains to King
Demos. The black coated advocates of spoliation
are not a nice lot."*

— DEAN WILLIAM R. INGE
ST. PAUL'S CATHEDRAL, LONDON

CHAPTER FIVE

A SURVEY OF THE SOCIAL ACTION LITERATURE

In the several decades since the end of World War I, a number of books have appeared which have profoundly influenced the Social Gospel, Social Actionist movement. Most of them have been books by men outside the church, and at least one by a man profoundly hostile to the church. But each one has in its own way added a plank to the platform of the churchmen who professed to be left of center. Of writers who wrote previous to these three decades, three names have been drawn upon heavily by theologians for their analysis and condemnation of what is called Capitalism. These three men are Karl Marx, Thorstein Veblen, the godfather of the New Deal, and Werner Sombart, who became a Nazi in 1933.

THE FABIANS

In addition to these three men, the writings of the various English Fabians have been exceedingly influential among churchmen, especially the work of R. H. Tawney, Sidney and Beatrice Webb, and G. D. H. Cole. Joseph Schumpeter, onetime Austrian minister of finance and later professor of economics at Harvard, in his book *Capitalism, Socialism and Democracy*, says of the Fabians that "the operative nucleus was bourgeois in background and tradition and also in another respect; most of its members were economically independent . . . They were careful about their facts which some of them took no end of trouble to collect by means of extensive research, and critical of arguments and measures. But they were quite uncritical as to the fundamentals, cultural and economic, of their aims. These they took for granted which is only another way of saying that, like good Englishmen, they took themselves for granted . . . Socialist endeavor of the Fabian type would not have amounted to anything at any other time. But it did amount to much during the three decades preceding 1914, because things and souls were ready for that kind of message and neither for a less nor a more radical one."

R. H. TAWNEY

The Fabian who exerted most influence in clerical circles is unquestionably R. H. Tawney, whose book *The Acquisitive Society* was published in 1921. This book is an analysis and criticism of a society so overborne by the lust to acquire material things that it has forgotten the ends which made material things worth acquiring. Tawney pursued this subject and only barely touched upon the most evil form which the acquisitive instinct takes, the political. If the lust to acquire material good by one's own unremitting toil is aesthetically bad, the lust to acquire the products of other men's toil by political manipulation is morally as well as aesthetically evil. Whenever government intervenes positively in the economy of a nation, the result is an economic advantage for some at the expense of others. A few men get something for nothing, the rest of the nation is forced to *part with* something for nothing.

Tawney touches upon this evil condition when he speaks of the "establishment of privilege as a national institution . . . (which) is the foundation of an inequality which is not accidental or temporary, but necessary and permanent. On this inequality is erected the whole apparatus of class institutions." Elsewhere he speaks about the "creation of a class of pensioners upon industry, who levy toll upon its product, but contribute nothing to its increase." And again he urges "the abolition of payments which are made without any corresponding economic service." To create understanding about the evils of privilege requires patient exposition; but the subject also lends itself well to moralizing and denunciation. Tawney has chosen the latter course. For the Fabian, privilege in itself is not an evil; the system of privilege works so well for the few that the Fabian wants everyone to have a political advantage over his neighbor!

An analysis of the acquisitive instinct which overlooks the nature of the state and makes no effort to analyze the political structures and means employed by the acquisitive instinct to gain its ends, typifies the glaring blind spot of the bulk of modern social thought.

Tawney's even more influential book *Religion and the Rise of Capitalism* appeared in 1926. The subject of the book is "the attitude of religious thought in England towards social organization and economic issues in the period immediately preceding the Reformation and in the two centuries which follow it." Tawney approaches his topic with tremendous historical erudition and a style spiced with wit, which ought to be a model for all who write on religious and social problems. Briefly, Tawney's thesis is that the Protestant Reformation created a climate in which a bourgeois capitalist organization of society could take root and grow. Tawney is a historian who tends to look down upon economics and, as a consequence, his work contains numerous thrice exploded economic fallacies. Ludwig von Mises has said that "The main *economic* fallacies of Tawney are: He does not realize 1) that capitalism has abolished all varieties of slavery, serfdom, indentured labor and so on; 2) that under capitalism (but not in the pre-capitalistic ages) the wage-earner is not only a producer, but at the same time the consumer of the much greater part of all things produced; 3) that the workers are the customers 'who are always right'; 4) that capitalism has raised the average standard of living (for a population eight or ten times as numerous as that of medieval England) in an unprecedented way; 5) that under capitalism the first concern of business (big business) is necessarily mass production for mass consumption."

WILLIAM TEMPLE

In 1928 William Temple, Archbishop of Canterbury from 1942 until his untimely death in 1944, published his volume *Christianity and the State*. The great political debate, insofar as that debate affects moral philosophy, is whether or not the men who comprise the political agency, or who act on behalf of government, are bound by the same moral code as men acting in their private capacity as citizens. In a socialized commonwealth the ruling elite cannot be fettered by the same moral code that guides the citizenry. If they are to act as they must in a planned economy, they must have a special moral dispensation. Temple deals with this situation and quotes the maxim "What is morally wrong cannot be politically right." He comments, "This maxim is usually intended, by those who make use of it, to declare that it cannot be right for the State to do what it would be wrong for an individual to do; and this is completely untrue. It shows a complete misunderstanding of the ethical problem to suppose that certain acts are right and certain other acts are wrong quite irrespective of the agent who does them and of the circumstances in which they are done."

It is also imperative in a planned economy that property be placed on a purely legal base and that moral sanctions for property be not allowed. On this matter Temple says, "What exactly the rights of property should be will vary according to many social conditions. But it is plain that the State, which gives sanctions to such rights, is fully entitled to determine what rights it will sanction, and is as completely at liberty to redistribute property as to protect its present owners in possession of it. But it must do this, as it should do all things, on moral principles and by moral methods."

MAX WEBER

An exceedingly influential work appeared in 1904 and 1905 in the German language, but it was not translated until 1930. This was *The Protestant Ethic and the Spirit of Capitalism* by Max Weber. Weber endeavors to show "the connection of the spirit of modern economic life with the rational ethics of aesthetic Protestantism." The book has a foreword written by Tawney, whose own work mines the same vein of ore as that of Weber. In his foreword Tawney writes about the pioneers of the modern economic order and says that the "tonic that braced them for the conflict was a new conception of religion, which taught them to regard the pursuit of wealth as, not merely an advantage, but a duty . . . Capitalism was the social counterpart of Calvinist theology." Weber himself is much more cautious in his assertions than Tawney and later authors in this field. Writing about the acquisitive instinct, he says "The impulse to acquisition, pursuit of gain, of money, of the greatest possible amount of money, has in itself nothing to do with capitalism. This impulse exists and has existed among waiters, physicians, coachmen, artists, prostitutes, dishonest officials, soldiers, nobles, crusaders, gamblers, and beggars. One may say that it has been common to all sorts and conditions of men at all times and in all countries of the earth, wherever the objective possibility of it is or has been given. It should be taught in the kindergarten of cultural history that this naive idea of capitalism must be given up at once and for all. Unlimited greed for gain is not in the least identical with capitalism, and is still less its spirit. Capitalism may even be identical with the restraint, or at least a rational tempering, of this irrational impulse."

Commenting on both Weber and Tawney, and their efforts to link capitalism and Protestantism, Charles A. Beard in his introduction to Brooks Adams' *Law of Civilization and Decay* writes that "it would have been well if later historians such as Max Weber and R. H. Tawney had pondered the problem which Henry Adams was pondering in 1897." Henry Adams had analyzed the economic mind as it had appeared long before the Reformation and had declared that in the late Middle Ages "the church itself had turned religion into a trade and made every priest a huckster." Later Lewis Mumford has somewhat corrected the one-sidedness of Weber and Tawney by relating certain Catholic monastic and medieval practices with modern capitalism. But the matter does not receive extended treatment.

Werner Sombart in his book *The Jews and Modern Capitalism* has attempted to do the same thing for the third great faith of the modern world. Sombart's book appeared in English in 1913 and was re-published by the Free Press in 1951. These works, which conjecture about the relation of a certain religion to a given economic order, undeniably provide diverting reading, but it is open to question as to how far they go beyond the stage of conjecture.

REINHOLD NIEBUHR

Somebody has said that the most intriguing title for a non-fiction work is Reinhold Niebuhr's *Moral Man and Immoral Society*, 1934. Niebuhr, professor at Union Theological Seminary in New York since 1928, bluntly states his thesis at the beginning: "The thesis to be elaborated in these pages is that a sharp distinction must be drawn between the moral and social behavior of individuals and of social groups, national, racial, and economic; and that this distinction justifies and necessitates political policies which a purely individualistic ethic must always find embarrassing." He believes that in society "Conflict is inevitable, and in this conflict power must be challenged by power." Moreover, the opposing factors in this conflict must make use of what Plato called the "Noble Lie." Niebuhr says "Contending factions in a social struggle require morale; and morale is created by the right dogmas, symbols and emotionally potent oversimplifications." Again, "Society must strive for justice even if it is forced to use means, such as self-assertion, resistance, coercion and perhaps resentment, which cannot gain the moral sanction of the most sensitive moral spirit." In the old debate as to whether or not the same code of ethics ought to bind the ruler as binds the ruled, Niebuhr seeks to provide a sanction for political conduct different from the sanctions of personal conduct.

The following year Niebuhr published his book *An Interpretation of Christian Ethics* at a time when he was strongly under the influence of Marxism. He says "This Marxian conception (of a revolutionary age, a secular millennium) is incidentally the fruit of both a profound religious feeling and of astute social observations. The paradoxes of high religion are in it and the actual facts of history substantiate it to a considerable degree . . . The program of the Marxian will not create the millennium for which he hopes. It merely will provide the only possible property system compatible with the necessities of a technical age."

In 1935 appeared Jerome Davis' *Capitalism and its Culture*. Davis taught at Yale, but did not attain full professorial status. When the University failed to renew his contract in 1937, there was an outcry among the so-called liberals that academic freedom had suffered at Yale. The phrase "academic freedom" had come to have a meaning which bore no relation to either word in the phrase. It had come to mean that if your ideas were right, that is "left," a school should be forced to hire you. In a long and closely packed book, Mr. Davis lumps together everything which he regards as wrong in our society and puts the label "Capitalism" on the lump. The book is not philosophical, but, read with discernment, it is not without interest.

Legalized Plunder

In 1936 Gustavus Myers' *History of the Great American Fortunes* was re-published. This had first appeared in 1909 and had acquired a considerable reputation as a type of the literature called, without disparagement, "muckraking." The reappearance of this three volume work in an inexpensive reprint insured its wide circulation. Myers was a Marxist, and, as the title of his book implies, he described the origin in the nineteenth century of American fortunes. His work is taken to be an indictment of capitalism and a demonstration of what happens when the economic processes are free from political controls. Later investigators have shown that on factual grounds Myers is not always reliable because his primary interest was in proving a case,[3] but even if we take Myers at face value, his book does not prove what he intends to prove, nor what those who rely upon it use it to prove. In the first place, it is simply not true that the eighteenth and nineteenth centuries were periods when economic life was free from political intervention. During Colonial days Myers speaks of "the crushing laws with which Colonial capitalists had to contend." Throughout the book he underscores, by continued repetition, the fact that the fountain source of every one of the great fortunes he condemns is a political privilege of some sort. Either the plunderers who gained a fortune received a special grant from Congress or some legislature or they conducted their predations having the foreknowledge that they would not be embarrassed by any legal action taken against them. Again and again Myers points out the care with which the plunderers secured the connivance of politicians. It is interesting to go through the volumes and underscore the passages which indicate that the plunderers realized "the importance of the principle that while it was essential to control lawmaking bodies, it was imperative to have as their auxiliary the bodies that interpreted law." In the first volume alone, I have underlined fifty-nine such passages. Myers also points out that if the acquisitive instinct exercised through political

---

[3] See especially "The Hall Carbine Affair." Wasson examines in detail one incident that throws considerable light on Myers' method and purpose. Also he shows that a number of highly touted social scientists have done little more than copy from Myers and from each other.

channels brought fortunes to some men, it was not lack of such an instinct but rather lack of similar opportunity, which caused others to lose out in the contest. He writes of our nineteenth century society, "Society has made money its God." Myers' book is an important study if read with the libertarian contention in mind that all exploitation, if analyzed, will reveal either that government is doing what government should not do, or that government is not doing what government should do. It is impossible to read this book and still refer to the laissez-faire capitalism of the nineteenth century. There was no laissez-faire.

In much the same vein as Myers' book is Ferdinand Lundberg's *America's 60 Families*, a study of the so-called Plutocracy. The date of Lundberg's book is 1937. The apostles of social change like to point to this book also as a revelation of what happens when government does not control economic affairs. But Lundberg says, "Government has been the indispensable handmaiden of private wealth since the origin of society. And far from having embellished history with a significant exception, the government of the United States, without the camouflage of custom or tradition, ritual or dogma, Church or Aristocracy, has actually done more to prove the truth of this generalization than have all the governments of Europe. So perfect, so thorough, has been the collaboration of politics and private fortune since the founding of the American colonies that it is difficult to ascertain from the data of any given period where political intrigue on behalf of specific private interest has terminated."

Neither Myers nor Lundberg includes every private fortune or accumulation of wealth in his indictment. Many men have become wealthy by producing goods or rendering services for which people willingly pay. But where wealth was accumulated by plunder, both authors, but especially Myers, reveal that the politician must necessarily be part of the plunderbund. The fact that Myers did not intentionally reveal this, and was, in fact, in favor of bigger government, makes his book all the more valuable for the libertarian. The collectivist who starts to analyze exploitation with the idea of passing a government remedy for it, is hoist on his own petard.

William Temple wrote *Christianity and the Social Order* for Penguin Books in 1942 in an effort to elaborate the non-economic religious criteria to which economics is properly subject. The book contains some ringing words on freedom such as, "On freedom all spiritual life utterly depends. It is astonishing and terrifying that the church has so often failed to understand this." But Temple concludes his book with an endorsement of a political program of public housing, public education, minimum income guaranteed by government, a government guaranteed voice in the conduct of business where the citizen works, and so on. These goals cannot be realized without a considerable impairment of freedom in each of the areas involved. Mere profession of devotion to freedom is nullified by embracing a program whose operational procedures are incompatible with freedom.

The Servile State

In the first few years of the second half century the older idealism of the Social Gospel has given way to thinking that seems to bear the marks of a cynical realism. Reinhold Niebuhr, who has so often been a bellwether in the social action movement, now commits himself flat-footedly to the idea that some men are good enough to rule other men and that the ruled are to consent for their own good. In his recent book *Christian Realism and Political Problems*, 1953, he criticizes St. Augustine's failure to "recognize the difference between legitimate and illegitimate, between ordinate and inordinate subordination of man to man." Niebuhr concludes, "Without some form of such subordination the institutions of civilization could not exist." This conjures up a picture of the servile state whose approach Hilaire Belloc foresaw and dreaded. That it should now be advocated as the norm of a Christian society is another of those ironies of history.

The cause of Socialism, Christian or otherwise, has enlisted some noble and generous spirits precisely because they saw in it a social ideal which would end the subordination of man to man. Now that this route has proved to be truly the "road to serfdom," there is the strongest possibility of an exodus which will leave the Christian social action movements solely in the hands of those who pursue the phantom of power.

HEADING LEFT

Any selection of books must be highly subjective, and there are undoubtedly omissions that some will regard as serious. In addition to those already mentioned, there are other important books, such as Harry F. Ward's *Our Economic Morality*, 1929, and *In Place of Profit*, 1933. The former is a virulent indictment of capitalism in terms of its alleged violation of the ethics of Jesus, and when the book appeared it gained extravagant praise from Reinhold Niebuhr and Jerome Davis. The latter book is a lengthy, on the spot study of incentives in a totalitarian state, Russia. In addition to being an appraisal of what keeps people going under communism, it trumpets the utopian fulfillment already accomplished under the Soviets, and the glory to come. Such an apologetic for communism takes the book out of the main stream of the Social Gospel.

Harry Ward's main influence has not been through his literary output, but through his teaching and his activities on behalf of organizing the churches for social action. Ward, English born, helped to found the Methodist Federation for Social Service in 1907. In 1912, Ward edited a book entitled *The Social Creed of the Churches*, which was one of the semi-official handbooks of the newly organized Federal Council of the Churches of Christ in America.

After several years on the faculty of the Boston University School of Theology, Ward accepted a post at Union Theological

Seminary in 1918. In 1941 he became emeritus. A generation of students came under his influence.

Another influential theologian at Union is J. Paul Tillich. He came to Union in 1934 after already attaining a European reputation, and has continued to grow in stature. After twenty years at Union he has announced his resignation and his acceptance of a post at Harvard University. Tillich's Religious Socialism is regarded as one of the important strands of his work. A comment on it by Nicholas Berdyaev in his book, *Christianity and Class War*, 1933, is worth noting. In writing of continental theologians, Berdyaev says, "the school of Karl Barth favors socialism, and the religious socialism of Tillich even sympathizes with communism."

Berdyaev, a Russian exile, deeply religious, a man of powerful mind and luminous insight, was nevertheless attracted deeply to Karl Marx. *Christianity and Class War* was dedicated to Marx, although Berdyaev now recognized Marx as his "fell enemy." As to social diagnosis, Berdyaev leaned heavily on Marx; they parted company when it came to recommending a cure.

An underlying premise of collectivism is that the natural human situation is one in which the hand of every man is raised against his brother. If the blow does not fall it is only because of the fear of retribution. The uneasy truce that does obtain in society is made possible only by the policeman. The warring elements would fly apart were they not held together by a strong government which keeps men from obeying their natural tendencies to injure each other and guides their energies into fruitful channels. The antisocial nature of man is the premise whether articulated or not, of all varieties of collectivism, those who have a mandate to rule, and have the coercive powers of government in their hands, will produce golden conduct out of these leaden impulses.

There is another theory of society. From Leibniz, through Adam Smith and Frederic Bastiat, there was emphasis on social harmony, the idea that "we are members, one of another." It was believed that the long range interests of members of society, rightly understood, do not conflict but are harmonious. Against this broad and deep background of social harmony there are occasional collisions of individual interest, and so to preserve the harmony a limited government is needed to punish individuals who trespass on the person or property of others.

Barely had Bastiat finished his *Harmonies of Political Economy* in 1849 when a rip tide came in from the other direction bearing the names of Darwin and Marx. With these men was relaunched the idea that nature was an arena with a struggle for existence going on ceaselessly, and that the moving force in history is the struggle of class against class. Once these ideas seep into the mind, social thought begins to include the idea of a necessary countervailing force in society powerful enough to suppress conflict and keep the warring elements in society in a condition of unstable armistice. The germ of the idea of the totalitarian state appears.

In other words, what has set the stage for omnipotent government in the modern world is the assumption that there is repressed conflict at the heart of society which would break out into open warfare like jack out of the box the moment the pressure is off the government lid. Therefore, build a heavier lid and apply more pressure! Berdyaev lends some of his weight to this attitude by saying, "Our sinful world is the scene of a conflict between opposed forces: this conflict determines the existence of the organic universe, it is the central fact of the social world of man . . . The class war in the social world is only one of the manifestations of this cosmic struggle and mutual antagonism; it can be seen also in opposition between the sexes and between nations." Obviously, this assumption cannot be dismissed casually, and Berdyaev is mentioned in this place to indicate his contribution to Christian social thought, and to recommend that this remarkable man be wrestled with.

Christian Ethics: New Style

In the background of the social actionist camp, another weapon was being readied. It was a new interpretation of Christian ethics. The older Christian ethics had upheld the position that right and wrong meant what they are commonly taken to mean; values that cannot be reduced to convenient and inconvenient, customary and uncustomary, legal and illegal. Emphasis in Christian ethics has now shifted to the needs of the neighbor. Instead of "Do what is right merely because it is right," the injunction now is, "Your obligation is to meet the needs of your neighbor" – overlooking the fact that doing right is also pragmatically the best way of meeting your neighbor's needs. The new concept of neighbor ethics is treated in a book by Paul Ramsay, *Basic Christian Ethics*, 1952.

This is a Christian ethic which fits admirably the needs of the proponents of the welfare state philosophy; every welfare state measure is justified by saying that it meets human needs and thus serves the neighbor, defined as the man in need. This curious interpretation of Jesus' commandment about loving our neighbor as ourselves, must practice discrimination on two levels. First, it must divide men up into two classes: neighbors and non-neighbors. The "neighbors" are to be subsidized by government handouts while the non-neighbors are to be taxed to provide the subsidy. Secondly, there is discrimination between the needs of even those selected as "neighbors." The "neighbor" may have illicit needs which even the most lenient welfare stater would be reluctant to put within the domain of government dispensations.

In 1953 there appeared a symposium entitled *Goals of Economic Life*, the first volume of a series of six to be issued under the direction of a study group authorized by the Federal Council of Churches in 1949. This series on the Ethics and Economics of Society is operating on a grant of nearly a quarter of a million dollars from the Rockefeller Foundation. Reinhold Niebuhr's contribution to this symposium may be cited as indicative of a trend to allow, grudgingly, that libertarians do have a case and are not merely the "minions of reaction," as Niebuhr once said. Speaking of "the debate about the limits and possibilities of a free economy," Niebuhr says, "Both sides in this ideological struggle obviously have hold of a truth which must be supplemented by the truth which the other side cherishes."

POLITICAL POWER – ECONOMIC ATTRACTION

In this book the so-called "economic power" argument appears in several of the contributions. Those who are worried about "economic power" and seek to balance it with political power have in mind, to use the words of John C. Bennett, "the prevention of any private centers of economic power from becoming stronger than the government as the political organ of the community."

The realm of the political is obviously the realm of power; the law can command police, jails, armies. The question is whether or not the possession of economic goods gives the possessor power analogous to political power. The word power is used in several different senses. There is, for example, a "power" by which a young lady of the theater impels young men to buy front row seats, but this is not analogous to the power which can conscript young men to die on a battlefield half way around the world. "Economic power" is more nearly analogous to the "power" of the box office attraction than to the power of government.

But even if one cannot see that there is a false analogy between economic power and political power, and argues that there is only one power having two facets, one economic, the other political – then, on the level of the power argument itself, we must decide whether or not it is better to have economic and political power in different hands, or in the same hands. If there are two foci of power, then those of us who are without either can play at the game of balancing one off against the other, allowing neither to become overly strong. But when the same set of hands that controls the police and the military also controls the money and means of production, then tyranny is as absolute as human inefficiency will allow.

———————————— ≫ ————————————

*"Resolved . . . a world of irresponsible, competing and unrestrained national sovereignties, whether acting alone or in alliance or in coalition, is a world of international anarchy. It must make place for a higher and more inclusive authority . . . We believe that military establishments should be internationally controlled and be made subject to law under the community of nations."**

— JOHN FOSTER DULLES' COMMISSION
FEDERAL COUNCIL OF CHURCHES, 1942

———————————— ≫ ————————————

*John Foster Dulles was Secretary of State during the administration of President Dwight Eisenhower. (Ed.)

CHAPTER SIX

THE CHURCHES AND THE UNITED NATIONS

The American people are practically unanimous in rejecting the idea of a state church. They would also reject the idea of a State Department church, if that proposition were put to them. It is not put to them in so many words, but now that John Foster Dulles has become, in effect, the spiritual adviser on foreign policy to the National Council of Churches, a number of churchmen in the ecclesiastical bureaucracy are working at the job of providing the State Department with a religious arm, even though this may be far from their intentions. They seek to throw the prestige of religion and the weight of America's church members behind the current brand of internationalism; and they propagandize without ceasing for the United Nations. In the minds of the more expansive members of the official cloth, the church and the UN stand or fall together. A denominational official, writing in an official publication, has said: "These attacks on the UN – as distinguished from friendly suggestions for improving it – are attacks on the Christian faith itself.[4] Pronouncements of the National Council of Churches are usually couched in more cautious terms, but they boil down to about the same conclusion.

Churchmen individually are well within their rights in supporting the UN, and there is no questioning the sincerity of those who try to find religious sanctions for that organization.

---

[4]Herman Reissig, in *Christian Community* as quoted in *Faith and Freedom*, May, 1953.

The logic of their position is quite clear, and may be framed as a syllogism: The UN is the only way to peace; the Church is for peace; therefore, the Church must give the UN its all-out support. To those who are knocked off their feet by this logic, there is nothing more to be said. If the only alternative to the UN is total war, then it is insanity to criticize or oppose it. But is this the case? Many thoughtful persons think otherwise. Some persons who sincerely long for peace are critical of the UN because they fear that – despite the noble aspirations of many of its votaries – the United Nations' concept contains the ingredients for bigger and holier wars. The mentality behind the UN pumps messianic pressure into the old dream of world empire which seeks to establish one world of (our) law. This means eventual collision with a coalition of powers who want to be outside our law because they too are gripped by the delusion of one world of (their) law. These are the ingredients of religious wars, and they are of satanic inspiration.

CHURCH AND STATE

The church has yielded periodically to the temptation of wedding itself to a political organization, so that when the organization is discredited the church suffers. Ever since Constantine the Church has been linked in shotgun unions with the state; it has made its accommodation to secular authority, and has sometimes usurped that authority. For the first several centuries of its existence the Christian church was a fellowship of love among those united in God, a new kind of life cherished within the decaying Roman Empire. But in the fourth century an alliance was effected between church and state, and many features of the old Roman Empire survived their graft onto a stock radically different from the original. Burckhart writes that Constantine "gave the clergy every possible guarantee of favor, even so far as a sort of participation in rule, and in return the clergy were the most devoted agents for spreading his power." The Dutch theologian, Heering, dates what he calls the fall of Christianity from this period. Such a church-state relationship may be political realism in the Machiavellian sense; it is not religious realism.

Rulership has never been entirely secular. Every state has had to invoke some kind of religious sanction for its operations. Political power is strengthened if the state has only one spiritual authority to deal with. Conversely, for a church that wants to gain the whole world there is a clear advantage in gaining access to the levers by which that world appears to be moved. The disadvantages of a church-state arrangement are not so obvious. But it always sets in motion a kind of Gresham's Law of the bad driving out the good. In the long run, instead of the state becoming Christian, religion becomes politicized. That is to say, it ceases to be religious!

WORLD POLITICAL ORDER

Thus it is to be expected that proponents of a world political order along the lines of the United Nations should seek to enlist the church's support. They meet with little resistance because among churchmen there is a vague "world-mindedness" which is labelled "internationalism." The secular idea of a world political organization is also labelled "internationalism," and the two radically different concepts are mingled in a confused combination. There is true internationalism in a religion with a world missionary outreach but it has nothing to do with politics. It is similar to the internationalism of free trade, free travel, and the free exchange of ideas. But this brand of internationalism is confused with the other variety which embraces a world political organization like the UN or world federal government.

In our time political schemes of redemption appear to many to hold more promise than religious ones, and in this instance the "world-mindedness" of Christianity has been pressed into the service of an international political structure. "The Churches of Christ in the United States," declares Walter Van Kirk, "are committed to the establishment of a world political order."[5]

Dr. Van Kirk is the executive director of the Department of International Justice and Good Will of the National Council of Churches. He held the same post under the old Federal Council of Churches. He has held the two jobs for thirty years. Thus, for a generation, Dr. Van Kirk's point of view on foreign policy is pretty close to that which is represented as the voice of the church. A sampling of his outlook is imperative if we wish to understand what is being foisted upon the churches as their duty toward the UN.

The sentence quoted above would be more accurate if Dr. Van Kirk had said that the spokesmen for the NCC are themselves committed and are trying to commit the churches to a world political order. "It could hardly be otherwise," he continues. "Christians are the divinely inspired propagandists of world community." It appears that, in the thought of Dr. Van Kirk and those in the NCC for whom he speaks, "a world political order" and "world community" mean the same thing. Actually, the two things are quite different; a political order presupposes community. It is one of the tragedies of our time that the faster the fabric of world community has disintegrated, the more frantic have been the efforts to patch it up with gerry-built political structures. Religion is an important factor in the building of world community, to the extent that world community is possible. Religion gave Christendom its unity; religion was noted by John Jay in *The Federalist* as

---

[5]Walter Van Kirk, in *The Church and Social Responsibility*, Richard Spann, editor, p. 220. Dr. Van Kirk recently clarified his position in a letter to *The Christian Herald*: "When I refer to a 'world political order' I do not mean 'world government' as that term is generally used. I think of the UN as a form of 'world political order.' As a matter of fact, I have been outspoken in my criticism of those who seek to amend the Charter for the purpose of transforming the UN into a 'superstate.' I believe that we will make greater progress toward peace through the UN as it is, without the member states yielding to that body the national sovereignty that would be required were the UN converted into a world government."

one of the factors which made the thirteen colonies a union so that federal government was feasible. But the NCC spokesmen are trying to use religion to prop up the UN by making it appear that the churches are solidly behind it. "Despite differences as to theology or doctrine," says Dr. Van Kirk, "the Christian community in the United States is practically unanimous in its judgment that nation states must surrender to the organized international community whatever measure of their national sovereignty is required to establish peace and justice on a global scale." This may be the tenor of pronouncements of the NCC, but does it accurately reflect the thinking of the thirty-five million for whom the NCC claims to speak, much less the churchmen outside the Council's orbit?

For a generation and a half it has been the fashion among intellectuals and publicists to be internationalists of the political variety, and the tyranny of fashion is a sociological fact of first rate importance. A period is characterized by certain ideas, because those who entertain ideas like to have their mental furniture in the mode. Intellectuals who live by selling words have discovered that if they want to drive a late model car they must hawk late model ideas; the market in old ideas is always slow. But the church has watched ideas and philosophies come and go. It should be relatively immune to intellectual fashions, able to resist the chance winds of doctrine, content to bear witness to its Truth. It should be an organization that is not afraid to condemn and rebuke popular enthusiasms while appealing to an older and deeper wisdom. Churchmen, however, are children of their age, and like to have their fellow intellectuals think well of them. Always in the past some churchmen have sought and found religious sanctions for every form of misgovernment and every evil that has plagued society; they are doing it today. Every age is penitent for the sins of its forebears; its own sins may have the surface appearance of virtues.

"Jesus and Geopolitics" is the exciting title of a chapter in one of Dr. Van Kirk's books. In it we read that "the Christians countered the geopolitics of Rome with a geopolitics of their own . . . With remarkable foresight they appropriated to their own ends the instruments of empire."[6] The intended parallel with our own times is easily grasped; Christians today, if they would emulate the ancient church, must appropriate the instruments of the UN for their own ends. Apparently, as Dr. Van Kirk reads the history of Christendom, the instruments of empire served the ends of religion. Shades of theocratic imperialism! The church barely survived its first marriage with empire, the second may do it in.

COMMUNITY OF NATIONS

Mr. Dulles was not always in the religious picture; he figures prominently in it now. Dr. Van Kirk began as a religionist who seeks to use the international political machinery of the UN for religious ends. Mr. Dulles, on the other hand, began as an internationalist who discovered a religious instrument that was already aimed at internationalist ends.

John Foster Dulles is the product of a Presbyterian manse, like another noted peaceworker, Woodrow Wilson. He has been part of the international political and commercial scene since the first World War, and of church political action since the late thirties. In 1937, Mr. Dulles attended a League of Nations sponsored conference in Europe and, as an ardent internationalist, was dismayed by the nationalistic bickering of the politicians assembled there. He left this conference to attend a similar one for churchmen held at Oxford. The churchmen appeared to be free from prejudices and nationalistic bias, and Mr. Dulles was delighted. He began to observe the ecclesiastical situation closely and found that churchmen had been working for years to prepare the ground for the acceptance of some kind of international political order as

---

[6]Walter Van Kirk, A Christian Global Strategy, p. 21.

a Christian imperative. This fact was enough to bring Mr. Dulles importantly into American church circles in 1941 as the first chairman of the Commission on a Just and Durable Peace of the Federal Council of Churches. His efforts to draft a set of principles on which peace might be built sounded to him, he said, like an echo of the Gospels.

Mr. Dulles resigned this chairmanship in 1949 to run for public office, but he still carries weight in official church circles. A recent issue of *Time* characterizes him as "a practical missionary of Christian politics." Whether this is so or not, it is a fact that Mr. Dulles, a lifelong internationalist, happened upon the church late in life and found in it an instrument admirably adapted to his purposes, an instrument with which he could and did work.

Just prior to Mr. Dulles' association with the Federal Council of Churches, in 1940, the first American Study Conference on the Churches and the International Situation met in Philadelphia and resolved that "the Churches, which in themselves transcend national frontiers, have a peculiar responsibility to help expand men's loyalties to include the whole number of the children of our Heavenly Father and the world government required by their common needs." Following up this lead, Mr. Dulles' Commission in 1942 held a conference at Delaware, Ohio. It resolved that "a world of irresponsible, competing and unrestrained national sovereignties, whether acting alone or in alliance or in coalition, is a world of international anarchy. It must make place for a higher and more inclusive authority . . . We believe that military establishments should be internationally controlled and be made subject to law under the community of nations."[7]

SOUND AND SILENCE

This is the line and there has been no deviation from it. In a recent official NCC pamphlet on the UN, Dr. Van Kirk writes:

---

[7]*Delaware Report*, pp. 11, 16.

THE LIBERTARIAN THEOLOGY OF FREEDOM

"Once the Allied armies had taken the offensive against Hitler, the churches took the initiative in demanding that an international organization be created to maintain the peace . . . They were among those who called for the establishment of the United Nations."[8] And the NCC continues to call for support of the UN, and brands those who question or oppose it for whatever reasons as unchristian and "isolationist."

Like the NCC, the World Council of Churches supports the idea of a world political order and officially supports the UN. The WCC endorsement of the UN intervention in Korea caused the withdrawal of its Chinese members, one of whom was a president of the WCC. The Evanston meeting of the WCC August 1955 favored the UN and resolved that "it is important that a dynamic concept of the world organization be kept alive and that the UN structure be subjected to periodic review." It urged that the UN "become more comprehensive in membership." It lamented that "little or no progress has been made toward world disarmament or the creation of an international police force."[9]

There are organizations set up for the sole purpose of propagandizing for the UN, such as the American Association for the United Nations. There are related organizations, such as the Church Peace Union and the Foreign Policy Association, doing a similar job. No one can quarrel with an organization that does what it is set up to do – even though one may wish to debate the merits of its case. It is different with the NCC. The NCC, according to its own literature, "is not something apart from the churches, but those churches themselves doing together those things which can be better done unitedly than separately." There is, therefore, a question of the propriety of an organization with this announced purpose becoming such a willing sound board for

---

[8]Walter Van Kirk, *The Churches and the United Nations*, p. 4.
[9]From Section IV of the official Evanston Report.

UN propaganda. In allowing itself to be so used the NCC has lost its effectiveness as an independent voice on moral issues.

During the past two decades there have been critically important moral issues in the international relations field. But on many of them, those of first magnitude, the churchmen in or close to the interdenominational hierarchy have neither raised their voices as individuals nor brought the issues within official purview. Here are some of the issues in which moral values were at stake and on which churchmen, with notable individual exceptions, were silent. First of all, those with no axe to grind, whose first devotion was to truth, would have striven during the late 1930's to keep open the debate as to whether or not the United States should participate in World War II. As will be recalled, what began as a debate degenerated into name calling as soon as the intellectuals were enlisted on the interventionist side. The pulpits of the land provided few nonpartisan voices calling the disputants to sanity and principle. In the second place, there was room for an evaluation in terms of ethics of the way in which the war was being fought. But a typical ecclesiastical reaction was the declaration of the Archbishop of Canterbury, just after a European city had been bombed out, that it would be a mistake to use too little force. Gerald Heard, commenting on this incident, remarked that the State begins to wonder if it is worth fifty thousand a year to keep a man to tell it that! Third, there was the atomic bombing of a people who had been trying for months to surrender, an act whose moral significance was largely ignored at the time.

In the postwar period, it would appear that the very minimum dictated by Christian principles would be an effort to encourage a full and free discussion of such matters as the expulsion of some eighteen million people from east Germany and Poland; the Stalin-White-Morgenthau Plan for the decimation of Germany; the war crimes trials in Europe and Japan; the attempt by "revisionist" historians to reopen the official accounts of WWII *that the truth may be known.* Instead, an impartial survey of the period must conclude that the preachers presented arms again, as did their predecessors in World War I, but more subtly this time and therefore more successfully – from the viewpoint of the State – and the establishment of World government through the United Nations became their next objective.

IDEAS HAVE CONSEQUENCES

After WWII, I began to sense the ways in which economics, politics and theology are mutually implicated; I understood for the first time why theology had once been called "The Queen of Sciences." I came to realize that many of the modern world's ills are due to the fact that politics (whose symbol is power) and economics (whose symbol is wealth) have usurped a role in our lives which borders on idolatry. This usurpation occurs because the western religious vision has dimmed; the dimension of transcendence is no longer a vibrant part of modern temper. Such are among the consequences of embracing certain unsound ideas popular during the past couple of centuries.

— THE REVEREND EDMUND A. OPITZ, 5/12/89

"Anthony, at the height of his sanctity, once asked the Lord, 'What of the other souls?' 'Anthony,' his Lord answered, 'I have given you your soul to save. The others are mine.' "

— GERALD HEARD,
AUTHOR

CHAPTER SEVEN

THE LIBERTARIAN THEOLOGY OF FREEDOM

We live in a time of widespread and well-founded apprehension. The sacrifices made during the Second World War, still so recent in our memories, did not result in the peace we were promised. Instead, by an incredible series of blunders and betrayals in high places we have been led to the brink of a Third World War, more terrible in prospect than the Second.

A WEAPON OF FREEDOM

The outcome of the Second World War was never seriously in doubt. The overwhelming preponderance of manpower was on our side, and the resources of wealth of the world likewise. The enemy in that war had a philosophy called Fascism. This philosophy had never been attractive enough to gain more than a few adherents in our land, and these were not people whom one could take seriously.

In the contest which looms on the horizon, the scales have shifted. The potential enemy has a preponderance of manpower, and he controls vast and important areas of the earth's surface. What is even more important, he has a philosophy which possesses a diabolical charm for the discontented of all lands. The enemy's agents have risen to top circles in our own government, and they are a menace even in those governments which they do not actually control. Against this giant we possess a Weapon, a few technological advantages, and a slight edge in the matter of freedom.

This essay won the Freedom Foundation's Bronze Medal. (Ed.)

THE ENEMY'S TRUMP CARD

The enemy's trump card is inducing us to become just like the thing we profess to be fighting against, which makes it impossible to win in principle.

But even if a sudden plague should remove forever this former ally turned enemy, our worries would not be over. We would then have to contend with an overgrown political establishment whose activities intrude into every aspect of our economy and frustrate individuals at a score of points. Our ancestors thought to protect their liberties and ours by placing constitutional limitations on the exercise of governmental power. But the Constitution is a thing of paper, no better than the men who interpret it. What the Constitution sought to prevent was personal government; it designed a government in which rulership would be of laws, not of men.

But a regime of personal government is now in vogue in almost every country in the world, including our own. The original balance of our system has been destroyed through the seizure of power by the executive and by the virtual deflection of the other two branches of our government. The decision to place our troops in Korea was not made by Congress, nor by the people.

Not only do we have a regime of personal government, but government has made itself relatively independent of the people. The power of the purse was once strong enough to curb even kings, but now the Executive holds the purse strings. The Income Tax Amendment* legitimatized the claim of government to all the wealth produced in the country in amounts fixed by itself. And as if that were not enough, the government confiscated gold, perfected a method of converting the public debt into paper dollars; and employs the device of inflation to dilute the value of our currency.

---

*See The Law That Never Was, Benson & Beckman. (Ed.)

COST OF INFLATION

As to what inflation is costing us, Congressman Buffett has recently pointed out that the holders of government bonds lost more of their savings during 1950 by the process of government engineered inflation than the entire country lost in all the bank failures between 1921 and 1933. Holders of United States Savings Bonds in 1950 lost $3,600,000,000. All losses by bank depositors from 1921 through 1933 totaled $1,900,000,000. All of this has been justified by the federal government in terms of a dubious economics, the central thesis of which is that the way to prosperity is not by production but by political spending of what has been produced by those who work.

THE UPPER CRUST OF "EXPERTS"

These unreasonable things have to be made plausible to people if the rulers are to remain in power, and so a new class has appeared whose function is to explain the unexplainable. Thus we have witnessed in our time the rise of a caste system, an upper crust of "experts," and a lower caste of just ordinary citizens. The average man, which means every one of us, is told that he cannot trust his own competence; the intelligentsia will tell him what to think; the bureaucratic elite will tell him how to act; the experts will bring up his children for him. The new Brahmin class has granted one concession to the average man – it is going to let him pay the bills, thus restoring to him a measure of dubious pride.

The forces arrayed against the individual are formidable. There is the worldwide Communist conspiracy endowing men with a fanaticism not witnessed since the Crusades. This is a creed for which men have lied, murdered, and betrayed their countries. It is a fraudulent internationalism cynically exploited by the men in the Kremlin on behalf of an expanding Russian nationalism. But the crisis is not in the menace of Communism.

Then there is the rise of personal government. The founders of this republic sought to protect individuals against their own government, because, as Woodrow Wilson said, "The history of liberty is the history of the limitation of government." In the American scheme the rights of each individual were to be protected by laws which even those in power were bound to respect. Now, officials are placed above the law. But the crisis is not in the rise of personal government.

A new kind of economics has come into vogue, whose role is to give personal government the means of disregarding popular will. It enables government to control its own purse strings and to create a seeming prosperity by multiplying the number of dollars and by piling up a debt that can never be repaid. But the crisis is not in the popularity of a false economics.

In desperation, the average man turns to the self-styled "experts," and a new intelligentsia arise who are nothing more than symptoms of the disease they are called in to cure. But the crisis is not the appearance of a new Brahmin class of "experts."

THE CRISIS IS WITHIN

The crisis is in man himself, in each individual regardless of his occupation, education, or nationality.

The crisis in each person is manifested in the feeling that the actions we take as individuals will have little or no effect. The individual no longer feels that he is master of his own destiny; instead he has been led to believe that a new kind of society has emerged in which the individual hardly counts at all. The mass has overcome the man. The individual seems dwarfed into insignificance – except as he becomes a part of some crowd or pressure group. It seems as if a man's two feet were given him not to stand on but to run with. So long as he runs with the pack he thinks that he is safe, but let him take a stand anywhere and he is in danger of being engulfed by the pack. The business of living has come to be the finding of ways to fit little men into big societies. So there is a tendency to play it safe, a tendency to adopt any sort of camouflage which will conceal – even from ourselves – the fact that each of us is a unique personality, responsible ultimately to his Maker.

THE CHANGE OF AMERICAN PSYCHOLOGY

The American psychology has changed. The self-reliance which lay back of the pioneering spirit has given way to a reliance on authority. It is one thing for the individual to be temporarily overcome by the sheer weight of numbers; it is something else again when the individual acquires a permanent psychology of subservience to the faceless mass, to government, to the "experts." Too many Americans have been taught *to know their place*; they have been confused by world events; they have accepted the contradictory promises of their leaders; they have surrendered their prerogatives. But now the seeds of revolt against this subservience are just beginning to sprout. There are evidences that we are beginning to look with a more critical eye upon what has been happening to us and the world during recent decades. If we look with sufficient penetration, we might come up with some answers. The search itself is part of the answer – and the key that unlocks the rest.

OUR DESTINY IS IN OUR HANDS

The question before all other questions is: How can we as individuals regain the conviction that our destiny is in our own hands? Questions of human destiny bring us face to face with the postulates of religion. The religion of Jesus was founded on two basic premises: first, "The Kingdom of God is within you" – or, "within your reach" and second, "The Kingdom of God is at hand" – now. This is the gospel, "the good news" to which the ancient world responded and to which we might respond again, now, anytime.

This generous estimate of the individual was the foundation upon which this republic was established. "Wherefore," said Thomas Paine, "political as well as spiritual freedom is the gift of God through Christ." You cannot found a republic on anything but free men; that was America's finest natural resource. The great Frenchman, DeTocqueville, noted this when he visited America in the 1830's. He wrote that the advantage of this country lay not in its harbors, its fields, forests, or rivers; not in its mineral wealth nor in its manufacture – but in its men.

They became a new breed with the discovery that they were free. DeTocqueville perceived the part religion had played in shaping this new kind of man when he wrote in *Democracy in America,* "Religion . . . is the first of their political institutions."

RESISTANCE IS THROUGH GOD

Because of his reliance on God the early American received direction from within; he did not need coercion from without. "Resistance to tyranny," he believed, "is obedience to God." So these men kept government at a distance and severely curbed the range of its powers. As a result of their freedom there was such a release of human energy as the world had not witnessed before.

We recognize the existence and operation of laws governing the physical world. Certain situations are invariably linked to predictable consequences. Each element and compound has properties which are natural to it. But the boundaries of the natural world do not stop where the realm of chemistry and physics ends. Freedom is just as natural a condition for man as warmth is of sunshine. "The God who gave us life," said Thomas Jefferson, "gave us liberty at the same time." Slavery of any degree is contrary to the nature of things. No individual is a mere appendage to anyone else; a man's soul is his own. "The Kingdom of God is within you," not in some men only, but in all men potentially.

Before any steps can be taken toward the recovery of a sense of significance and responsibility, the individual must become aware of the fact that he is a person in his own right, responsible for his gift of life to the Source of his being. But in our time events have conspired to make it difficult for the individual to come to this realization. Life has become so complex that it seems as if the person must bow down before mere numbers.

This is a superstition.

The first step in recovery must be to destroy the superstition that the mass is superior to the man. The delusions which disfigure our thinking about society and government are the principal threat to the individual, because it is in these two areas that the force of numbers seems to be most compulsive.

DOES MAN EXIST FOR SOCIETY?

It is claimed by "advanced" thinkers that the decline in importance of the individual is the natural, and desirable, consequence of the increasing complexity of society. The individual, in this point of view, is not justified in living his own life; he should dedicate himself to the welfare of the group – as the group welfare is defined for him by one of the "experts." Under simpler conditions, they say, society may have existed for man, but now man exists for society. If the good of society demands it, the individual may be sacrificed.

WHAT IS SOCIETY?

These are the claims. What are the facts? The fact is that there is no such thing as Society, spelled with a capital S – there are only persons! Society with a capital letter is an idol we ourselves have fashioned, or which a few men have constructed to give them a plausible excuse for ordering other individuals around. Society is nothing but the persons who compose it, and the character of any society is determined by the quality of the individuals in it. If the individuals are decent, kind, and intelligent, it is a good society. If they are warlike, the society is martial. If they can be persuaded that black is white, it is a superstitious society. You cannot get golden conduct out of leaden impulses, and you can't make a good society out of bad people.

Society is composed of individuals, each of whom is seeking to better his circumstances by cooperating freely in a variety of ways with his fellow man. Voluntary association is the essence of society, and it is in the voluntary associations we form for a variety of purposes that each of us realizes the fullness of his personality. We have no inclination to be hermits; we are social creatures, and we achieve our full humanity only in association, in mutuality, and in community.

Voluntary association is natural to man, essential to his development, but it withers and dies in the presence of compulsion. Compulsory association is the denial of society.

It appears harmless to urge that the person should dedicate himself to the welfare of the group. No one reflecting on the matter can fail to see that the welfare of the group cannot be at variance with the well-being of the individuals who compose the group. But the admonition is dangerous when the person making it implies that some one be given the privilege of defining the welfare of the group and the power of forcing individuals to submit. *This is the usual meaning of social reform.*

SOCIETY SHOULD BE REFORMED

An incalculable amount of harm has been done by those who have gone forth to reform society. As a matter of fact, there is no way of reforming society except by making individuals better. And no one can make individuals better except the individual himself. If you want to be a reformer – reform yourself. That will keep you busy for a while and lend encouragement to others. Then, when there are significant numbers of transformed individuals, society will be reformed – but not before.

The second superstition about mere numbers concerns our conceptions of government. There are those who admit that it just doesn't make sense to say that each individual member of society counts for nothing in himself, but if you add him to a hundred and fifty million other blanks you get something wonderful – Society with a capital S. To say that the individual is nothing, society everything, is not even a thinkable proposition. "But," say some, "that is where government comes in. The individual is a cipher, and a half-dozen ciphers side by side are still zero. But put a significant figure in front of them and you have a million. This significant figure is the Leader, the Dictator, the Ruler – representing government."

Those who hold this view admonish us to forget about the individual, forget about society; it is government which binds us all together and gives us stature. From this perspective, government becomes the all-pervading influence within which we live and move and have our being – usurping the place in thought once occupied by the God concept. Caesar and God have changed places. God is allowed a little time on Sunday morning, but it is Caesar who takes care of you during the rest of the week. It is government which protects us against the vicious foreign foe, turns production into prosperity, causes crops to grow, grants us security, and gives us the benefits of progress in the arts and sciences.

WHAT IS GOVERNMENT?

These are the claims. What are the facts? When the average person thinks of the word Government with a capital G, he sees in his mind's eye a vision of Uncle Sam hovering in the murky atmosphere over the White House. To dispel this image, visit any city hall, any state capital, or the national capital. There you will find not Government with a capital G but only people. Examine any of the vast proliferating bureaus or departments of government, and what you see are only more people – each of them spending half his time undoing the tangles caused by the way he spends the rest of his time.

There is no such thing as Government with a capital G. There is only an arrangement which sets aside a small group of people and gives them the power to coerce all the rest of the people.

A NECESSARY EVIL

The best that our Founding Fathers could say about government was that it is a necessary evil, and they devised the best scheme ever invented to limit the government's monopoly of compulsion to a minimum.

The great 19th century English statesman, John Bright, once remarked that he had known Parliament to do many good things – but never on purpose! The essence of government is power – the power of a few men over many men. Our daily experience tells us that power over other people is seldom used wisely. Lord Acton reminded us that all power tends to corrupt, and that absolute power corrupts absolutely.

There is a place for government in the affairs of men, and our Declaration of Independence tells us precisely what that place is. The role of government is to protect individuals in their God-given individual rights. Freedom is the natural birthright of man, but all that government can do in behalf of freedom is to let the individual alone, and it should secure him in his rights by making others let him alone.

THE ROLE OF GOVERNMENT

The role of government is to protect the voluntary associations which men, acting freely, form to further their private ends. Every man has equal freedom to follow the dictates of his own conscience, and government has no mandate to interfere unless some other man's equal claim to freedom is being impaired.

The men who wrote the Declaration were not anarchists – far from it. They conceived a government which was to be, in its concern for justice, more vigorous than any government had ever been. They wanted the function of this government limited to the protection of the equal rights of every man in freedom, not coming into play except when some individual trespassed on these rights of another. Within the limits set by a Higher Law they wanted government to be virile and alert; but they erected safeguards that were intended to prevent government from stepping outside these limitations.

They were much wiser than we are in later years. In our time we have given Caesar all power, and yet somehow we expect that power to set limits upon itself. This is fantastic. The corrupting influence of power is such that the men who comprise government desire ever more extensive powers over other men, and they will promise the most extravagant things in order to induce innocent and trusting persons to grant it to them. The terrible thing is that these extravagant promises are believed, with the result that more and more people are backed into the position of believing that they are mere creatures of the state – whereas they once considered themselves sons of God. Such is the progress of human enlightenment!

CLAIMS OF GOVERNMENT

It takes but a moment's reflection to convince ourselves that the preposterous claims of government are sheer fraud. Take, for example, the matter of economic security. The government promises to provide us with at least a minimum of economic goods – houses, food, clothing, and so on. Now, no person can give away what he does not possess, and neither can government. Government does not produce the economic goods it promises to dispense, nor is it a factor in their production; people do the producing. The three factors in production are land, labor, and capital; government is not one of these. Before government can give you anything, it must first take it away from somebody else; or, before it can give somebody else anything, it must first take it away from you.

This is not the way to either prosperity or justice. In current theory, government promises to be a Robin Hood, robbing the rich to pay the poor. This theory is immoral, but the practice is even worse. The promise is soon forgotten, and Robin Hood robs the rich and poor alike to pay Robin Hood.

CORRUPTION IN HUMAN SPIRIT

By trying to be all things to all men, government has usurped a place in the affairs of men to which it is not entitled. Caesar has boot-strapped himself into a false god. This is not a case of mere dishonesty or corruption in politics; this is a case of corruption in the human spirit. This is idolatry. And of all idolatries, worship of Caesar is the worst because it reduces persons to subjects.

We have spoken of the superstitions that clog our thinking about society and government. These superstitions are only symptoms. The real trouble lies deeper. The trouble begins with our nonreligious view of life, which declares that man has obligations only to his fellow men as they comprise society or government. This view of life is very much in earnest about rendering unto Caesar the things which are Caesar's. It is so very earnest about this that there is nothing left over to render unto God the things that are God's.

This view of life is not realistic because it ignores one entire dimension of life. It is not enough for man to have what we might call horizontal relations with his fellow men; his nature also demands what we might term a vertical relation with the Reality men call God. It is the fundamental premise of religion that each man has a relation to the heart of Reality which overshadows in importance his relation to any merely human creation. Where any human creation such as society or government usurps this place and assumes primacy, there is idolatry.

Not only is the prevailing view of life unrealistic, but it is also impractical. Look at the mess we are in! If your equation has only two terms, man and society, then it is logical that society, the sum of individuals, be superior to any given individual who is a mere fragment of society. The tyranny of mass over man is assured if you have only two terms. But with the three terms, God, man and society, the situation is changed. Every individual is then linked to a higher Reality and becomes a person in his own right with prerogatives that his society may not transgress.

WE MUST HAVE A REALITY
Unless there is a Reality superior to any human creation, which man can know, and with which he comes into contact in the deepest part of his being – unless there is a Beyond that is Within – what becomes of human freedom and the human conscience?

If the state sets itself up as the supreme arbiter of human affairs, it must domesticate the individual lest any lingering remnants of self-reliance weaken the state's authority. The state must restrict the individual's effort to follow the dictates of his conscience, lest they conflict with the decrees of Caesar. In the interests of its own safety the state must eventually deny that the individual is a person, for the individual can be a person only when he puts his obligation to God ahead of his obligation to Caesar.

The demand that our nature puts upon our life is that we finish our creation and complete our evolution by coming to terms with the Source of our being. This is why man is incurably religious, and why no tyranny has been able to suppress religion for long. Man has larger capacity than is demanded of him by the ritual of politics. Communism comes closest to replacing religion because it offers a fraudulent faith of its own, promising a secular scheme of redemption entirely within the social order. But in trying to further this scheme Communism must employ violence and systematic terror.

WE ALL ARE A PART

Here we have the pathetic situation of a hundred million adult persons, more or less, each one stultified by the feeling that he can't do anything about society, or government, or world conditions. There is pathos here because each one of us is part of the problem which every other one of us feels is insurmountable. If even ten percent of us would change our perspective ever so slightly, so that we would start doing the one thing which is already in our power to do – change ourselves – then the monster problems before which we feel so impotent would be deflated to man-size. This is not a process of wishing away our difficulties, but rather it is an honest effort to assess our problems for what they really are. The difficulties we can cope with are not problems so much as they are opportunities; we grow in stature as we encounter the things that brace themselves against us. World problems won't be solved by the world; they will be broken down and solved, if at all, by persons. Problems of the individual can be solved only by the person concerned, each one seeking such help as he deems necessary.

MAN WILL LOSE CONTENT

But even where some totalitarian regime tries to wipe out religion, we may confidently predict that man will not long be content with the exclusively horizontal relations he has with society and the state; there is something in him which demands a vertical relationship with Reality.

It is with this demand of our own nature that we should align ourselves, and it is possible to take this step anytime. The Kingdom of God is within you – and it is now. The obligation to realize this potential rests upon us as individuals and calls for an individual commitment. It calls for nothing less than facing of the facts about ourselves and our situation, and then appropriates action based upon the understanding we have thus gained.

THE CHOICE IS OURS

The recovery of a sense of responsibility and significance is up to us, and when we are no longer content with patchwork remedies and makeshifts, there will be this recovery. The choice is always ours. When we have made that choice, society will be reformed by the presence within it of transformed individuals. But the job of transforming individuals is something no one else is qualified to do for us; only we can do it for ourselves. And it is something we can start doing right now.

Notes:

About The Author

Edmund A. Opitz is an ordained Congregational minister, whose career as a spokesman for libertarian Christians, is now in its 5th decade.

Reverend Opitz left his parish in Beverly, MA, in 1945 to serve with the Red Cross in India. Upon his return, he served a parish in Hingham, MA until 1951, when a group of libertarian Christians asked him to become a director of Spiritual Mobilization, an organization formed to fight for the teachings of Jesus versus socialist concepts of the "Social Gospel."

In 1955, Opitz joined The Foundation for Economic Education, founded in 1946 by his friend Leonard Read. He remained at FEE as a staff member, lecturer, and associate editor of *The Freeman*, until his retirement in 1992.

Realizing that ministers needed to know more about economics to refute socialism, and that libertarian ministers needed to meet fellow ministers who believed as they did, Rev. Opitz founded The Remnant – a fellowship at whose meetings Opitz featured various well known free market economists.

Opitz was also a founder of the Nockian Society – a fellowship which seeks to maintain the availability of the works of Albert J. Nock.

To-date, over 150 major articles written by Opitz have been published in scores of publications and four books. His book-length treatise of the relationship between the Christian religion and free market economics was published under the title of *Religion and Capitalism: Allies Not Enemies*.

*In May of 1989, Ed attended the 50th Anniversary Reunion of his
seminary class and gave the following synopsis of his career:*

OBITER DICTA

My college major was political science; economics
was my minor. I had only the vaguest of notions as to
what I might do with these two disciplines; it just happened that they interested me – as did religion and
theology. So, after college, I enrolled at Andover New-
ton; I spent the most satisfying year of my academic
life on The Hill. It was only wanderlust which took
me to California, to the Pacific School of Religion in
Berkeley. Following graduation I served a few years of
apprenticeship in two churches, then went to India
with the Red Cross.

After World War II, I accepted a call to The Second Parish in Hingham. I began to sense the ways in
which economics, politics and theology are mutually
implicated; I understood for the first time why theology had once been called "The Queen of the Sciences."
I came to realize that many of the modern world's ills
are due to the fact that politics (whose symbol is power)
and economics (whose symbol is wealth) have usurped
a role in our lives which borders on idolatry. This usurpation occurs because the western religious vision has
dimmed; the dimension of transcendence is no longer
a vibrant part of the modern temper. Such are among
the consequences of embracing certain unsound ideas
popular during the past couple of centuries.

There are better ideas at hand. It is a great truth
that theistic religion makes sense out of the universe,
supplies clues as to man's nature and destiny, links the

individual conscience to the moral order, and invests life with meaning and purpose. It offers overall coherence. When true religion becomes fully operative in the lives of people, economics has the important but modest role of supplying our creaturely needs efficiently; politics strives for ordered freedom in society with "liberty and justice for all." Other sectors of life then respond to man's intellectual and spiritual hungers – for God, beauty, truth and goodness.

I was offered an opportunity to test out some of these ideas in the arena. It sounded exciting. I left my parish, fully intending to return in a couple of years. But it was not to be; there was always one more thing I needed to do, something I had to finish; which is why I have spent the last several decades at The Foundation for Economic Education in Irvington, New York. While there I coordinated the program for an informal clerical fellowship called The Remnant, took part in more than two hundred seminars, gave a lot of speeches and sermons, and published something like half a million words in articles and books. It's been bracing!

EDMUND A. OPITZ
MAY 12, 1989

Publisher's Note: When, in 1955, a number of Congregational churches refused to join the merger with the United Church of Christ, they lost their seminary affiliations and Edmund Opitz took on the job of helping to develop alternatives. "Ed's group" now consists of over 400 autonomous congregations who formed the National Association of Congregational Christian Churches, with executive offices in Oak Creek, WI. Oh yes – should you visit Cape Cod and hear of a band concert, you may see Ed, now 85, playing his beloved French horn.

Index

153

In 1963, Reverend Opitz together with Robert Thornton and A.H. Aring, founded the Nockian Society. We herewith present the writings of Albert J. Nock, which may be ordered through any bookstore or directly from us, Hallberg Publishing Corporation.

"This is the kind of book that gets under a person's skin, performing catalytically to persuade the reader into becoming what he has it in him to be."

— Edmund A. Opitz

ISBN 0-87319-038-6
352 pages, Trade Paper, $16.95

An essential history of Colonial America and must reading for students of government and advocates of man's right to Life, Liberty and Property.

ISBN 0-87319-023-8
112 pages, Trade Paper, $9.95

Albert J. Nock (1870-1945) was a radical, in the venerable sense of the word: one whose ideas cut to the root and make you think again about things previously taken for granted.

ISBN 0-87319-041-6
224 pages, Trade Paper, $14.95